New Directions for
Child and Adolescent
Development

William Damon
EDITOR-IN-CHIEF

Culture and
Developing Selves:
Beyond Dichotomization

Michael F. Mascolo
Jin Li
EDITORS

D1523392

Number 104 • Summer 2004
Jossey-Bass
San Francisco

CULTURE AND DEVELOPING SELVES: BEYOND DICHOTOMIZATION
Michael F. Mascolo, Jin Li (eds.)
New Directions for Child and Adolescent Development, no. 104
William Damon, Editor-in-Chief

Microfilm copies of issues and articles are available in 16mm and 35mm, as well as microfiche in 105mm, through University Microfilms Inc., 300 North Zeeb Road, Ann Arbor, Michigan 48106-1346.

ISSN 1520-3247   electronic ISSN 1534-8687

NEW DIRECTIONS FOR CHILD AND ADOLESCENT DEVELOPMENT is part of The Jossey-Bass Education Series and is published quarterly by Wiley Subscription Services, Inc., a Wiley company, at Jossey-Bass, 989 Market Street, San Francisco, California 94103-1741. Periodicals postage paid at San Francisco, California, and at additional mailing offices. Postmaster: Send address changes to New Directions for Child and Adolescent Development, Jossey-Bass, 989 Market Street, San Francisco, CA 94103-1741.

New Directions for Child and Adolescent Development is indexed in Biosciences Information Service, Current Index to Journals in Education (ERIC), Psychological Abstracts, and Sociological Abstracts.

SUBSCRIPTIONS cost $90.00 for individuals and $195.00 for institutions, agencies, and libraries.

EDITORIAL CORRESPONDENCE should be sent to the Editor-in-Chief, William Damon, Stanford Center on Adolescence, Cypress Building C, Stanford University, Stanford, CA 94305.

Jossey-Bass Web address: www.josseybass.com

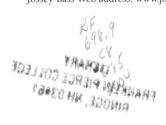

CONTENTS

EDITORS' NOTES

In recent years, scholars have looked to different cultures for alternatives to predominant Western conceptions of self. In so doing, psychologists often invoke the individualism-collectivism (I-C) distinction as an important source of cultural variation in self. From this framework, individualist (most Western) cultures are those that emphasize individuals as separate, autonomous, and self-contained entities. In contrast, collectivist cultures (most non-Western cultures) place primary value on group orientation, the goals and needs of others, and readiness to cooperate (Greenfield and Cocking, 1994; Hofstede, 1980; Markus and Kitayama, 1991; Triandis, 1994). Corresponding to individualist cultures, individual selves are seen as having sharp and well-defined boundaries but loose ties between individuals; the individual is expected to look after himself or herself. In contrast, in collectivist cultures people are born into cohesive in-groups and are obligated to honor relationships; selves exhibit permeable or loose boundaries.

It is important to preserve a distinction between the cultural and individual levels of analysis. The I-C distinction, as originally introduced by Hofstede (1980), is a construct pertaining to the *cultural* level of analysis, reflecting properties of cultures, not individuals. Many scholars have worked to identify the implications of I-C for selves at the *individual* level of analysis. For example, Triandis (1994) invoked the terms *idiocentric* and *allocentric* to refer to the types of selves that people construct in individualist and collectivist cultures. Others have made similar distinctions. In their now-classic work, Markus and Kitayama (1991) contrasted the notion of an *independent* self that arises in Western cultures with an *interdependent* self that arises in Asian cultures.

The I-C distinction has been useful in researching both similarities and differences in self across cultures (Kim and others, 1994; Markus and Kitayama, 1991). Triandis (1994) outlined a total of sixty-six possible distinctions between the allocentric and idiocentric selves. He hypothesized for allocentric selves that (1) groups rather than individuals are the basic units of social perception, (2) the behavior of others is explained using social norms rather than personal characteristics, (3) emotions are more likely to be other-focused than self-focused, (4) cognitions about self are focused more on what makes the self similar to the in-group than on what makes the self different from the group, and (5) cognitions are context-specific rather than context-independent. Empirical research based on the I-C framework did verify several of these hypothesized cultural differences in self (Oyserman, Coon, and Kemmelmeier, 2002).

1

Issues for an Analysis of Culture and Self in Development

The I-C dimension has been useful in generating and interpreting research about differences in self from a variety of the world's cultures. Despite their utility, invocation of differences also engenders a series of conceptual and empirical risks.

The Risk of Cultural Reification. First, with regard to the study of culture, the use of the I-C dichotomy runs the perennial risk of characterizing different cultures and the selves as *monolithic* entities. From this view, some cultures would be seen as individualistic, others as collectivistic, and still others lying between these extremes. Such a demarcation ignores the many textured ways in which I-C can manifest itself in a given culture, or even how a single culture can contain individualist and collectivist elements simultaneously.

Second is the obvious risk of *reductionism*. It is a common practice to identify a culture in terms of a single numerical value expressing its degree of I-C. The vastness and nuances of a cultural orientation (Kim and others, 1994) with regard to the I-C dimension then becomes reduced to a single point. If one were to follow such a reductionist approach, cultures could readily be reclassified as many distinct dimensions, such as scientism versus supernaturalism, authoritarian versus authoritative orientation, and so forth. By reducing complexity of culture to such distinctions, we may defeat rather than serve the purpose of studying cultures. Some scholars have proposed that it is more fruitful to view I-C as coexisting tendencies in any culture (Kagitçibasi, 1994; Sinha and Tripathi, 1994), which may help research move beyond the I-C model.

Third, many cross-cultural analyses tend to treat culture as an *independent variable*. As such, *nation* often becomes the operational definition of culture. Although this treatment of culture may be a useful research strategy, it has less utility to simply view culture as a discrete independent variable (especially viewed as external to individuals). Such a practice perpetuates the risk of reifying cultures as monolithic entities. Not only may there be many cultures within any given nation, cultural meaning systems themselves may contain divergent and sometimes conflicting meanings for representing aspects of self. As such, it might be best to think of any given "culture" as defined in terms of myriad consensual frameworks that fit together like a complex mosaic rather than as a unified structure.

Fourth, the use of culture as an independent variable tends to privilege *etic* over *emic* analyses of culture. An etic analysis attempts to compare cultures in terms of universal dimensions. An emic analysis explores the indigenous or culture-specific aspects of a given culture. Although valuable, etic analyses tend to obscure indigenous cultural meanings that do not translate well into universal views or those from without (Misra and Gergen, 1993). In doing so, emic analyses of culture are often eclipsed by the universalizing lure of etic approaches.

Dichotomizing Conceptions of Selves. Some of the same issues arise when we consider the concept of self as spawned by many cultural frameworks. When analyzing the development of self within cultural groups, there is the risk of conceptualizing different cultures as distinct and monolithic entities. Some scholars, especially those who adopt postmodern orientations, make sweeping claims about the nature of the purportedly independent and interdependent selves across cultures. For example, Hampson (1982) asserted "the Chinese concept of individuality has no room for a private self" (p. 189). Alternatively, Sampson (1989) characterizes the Western conception of self in terms of *self-contained individualism*. He suggests that the Western "concept [of self] describes a fictitious character. . . . whose integrated wholeness, unique individuality and status as a subject with actual powers to shape events has become null and void" (p. 3). Thus, on one extreme the Western self is depicted as the ideal of a self-contained character who sets himself or herself rigidly apart from social world; on the other extreme the members of entire non-Western cultures are characterized as devoid of any coherent experience or conception of an individual self.

We suggest that the dichotomization of human cultures and selves fails to capture the nuances and textures of cultures and the multiplicity of the selves in development. We suggest that traditional concepts of individualism tend to gloss over how interdependent, relational, and hierarchical selves develop within Western cultures. Likewise, concepts of collectivism limit how representations of individuality develop and function in non-Western cultures (Misra and Agarwal, 1985). There is a need for a more nuanced treatment of culture and self.

Beyond Dichotomization: The Multiplicity of Selves Between and Within Cultures

This volume is organized around the premise that neither cultures nor individuals are monolithic entities. It is not fruitful to view some cultures or selves as simply individualist or collectivist, even if such themes loom large within any given culture. Individuals in all cultures exhibit needs and concerns for individuality and relatedness. As such, all cultures must deal simultaneously with the *universal concerns* of individuality and communal relatedness. Nonetheless, because of the particularities of sociocultural and historical developments, members of diverse cultural groups construct ways of representing individual selves within social relationships in relation to each other. Thus cultures and the selves that develop within them can be said to exhibit "universality without uniformity" (Shweder and Sullivan, 1993).

Against this backdrop, selves are expected to exhibit a multiplicity of concerns, embracing both individualist and collectivist themes—not only *between* cultures but also *within* cultures. The contributors to this volume do not focus on dichotomizing nations or cultures. Instead, they strive to analyze similar and different ways in which individualist and collectivist themes make up the particular meanings espoused by members of each group under study. In this mode of analysis, culture is viewed as a set of emergent, consensual meanings that frame how individuals within a given social group interpret themselves, others, and their relationships. As such, cultural meanings are emergent rather than fixed, are distributed within and between individuals rather than outside of individuals, and evolve as new social problems arise and as individuals attempt to address them.

It is important to point out that, with some exceptions (for example, Greenfield and Cocking, 1994), researchers who adopt the I-C framework rarely consider the perspective of human development. This neglect has resulted in the fossilized products of development–outcomes whose developmental origins and pathways remain unexamined. This obscures an understanding of how the outcomes of development have been formed over time within particular cultural practices and contexts. All the contributors to this volume take a developmental approach to their particular research.

The contributors to this volume present empirical research from a number of cultures: the United States, China, India, and a variety of ethnic populations in the United States. All the contributors employed a combination of qualitative and quantitative methodology. They made attempts not to privilege qualitative over quantitative methodology or emic over etic analyses, but to regard these approaches as complementary and mutually informing. Finally, within their diverse topics, these contributors conclude by addressing explicitly the implications of their research findings for rethinking selves within and across cultures as well as for future research.

In Chapter One, "Individual and Relational Conceptions of Self in India and the United States," Michael F. Mascolo, Girishwar Misra, and Christopher Rapisardi report the results of their cross-cultural comparison of selves in urban areas of India and the United States. By using a set of multistep and multilayered methods, they interviewed respondents about how they experienced themselves with a variety of social partners. To classify the verbal protocols, the investigators developed a multidimensional Self-Facet by Relational Orientation model of self-experience. Six categories of self-facets were identified (emotions, self-evaluations, communications, intimacy relations, dependency relations, and personal dispositions). Each class of self-facets is further classified into four *relational orientations* (descriptions of self, mutual relations, self relating to others, and others relating to self). The resulting matrix is an etic framework for comparing descriptions of self. By analyzing the specific meanings provided by Indian and American participants, the investigators were able to identify a series of local emic meanings with the larger etic framework. Differing patterns of individual and relational orientations emerged for Indian and American samples. On the basis of their findings, the authors proposed a series of four modes of self-experience that may coexist in any given culture.

In Chapter Two, "Self in Learning Among Chinese Children," Jin Li and Xiaodong Yue examine how Chinese adolescents conceive of themselves as learners. Li and Yue's focus on learning as an important domain of self-conception was informed by the Confucian emphasis on learning as a process of moral self-perfection. Rather than approaching their research using an etic measure of an abstract variable (such as the I-C dimension), Li and Yue argue for the importance of representing the actual (emic) meanings that individuals within a given culture hold for themselves. Toward this end, in their first study the researchers used open-ended methods to collect written protocols about adolescents' learning goals. There was a greater tendency for Chinese adolescents to describe individual rather than social learning goals. In addition, participant protocols yielded a rich network of indigenous meanings that Chinese adolescents use when representing the activity of learning. In a second study, drawing upon these meanings, the researchers presented Chinese adolescents with a series of statements about learning. Participants were asked to rate the statements with regard to their individual versus social tendencies. Again, adolescents exhibited a higher level of individual than social orientation. The results suggest that Chinese adolescents exhibit a strong individual orientation to learning that must be taken into consideration in any attempt to understand Chinese conceptions of self.

In Chapter Three, "Multiplicity of Ethnic Identification During Middle Childhood," Daisuke Akiba, Laura A. Szalacha, and Cynthia T. García Coll address multiplicity of ethnic identity among American immigrant children. They suggest that ethnic identity, as an important part of the self, has been traditionally approached in a "social vacuum." The accuracy or the strength of an individual's ethnic identification has been assessed with reference to the ethnic group to which investigators have assumed individuals objectively belong. Alternative dimensions are rarely considered. The authors propose that in today's more-diverse-than-ever societies, ethnic identification may be better defined in terms of (1) how individuals identify themselves with reference to a variety of social groups and dimensions and (2) how they make sense of these multiple memberships. Their in-depth interviews with more than four hundred children immigrant families indicate that young children use a variety of personal and social categories to construct their ethnic identity, among them identifications in terms of native language, cultural background, gender, race, and various personality characteristics. This research supports their argument for the multiplicity of identity formation among immigrant children.

In Chapter Four, "Within-Culture Complexities," Catherine Raeff argues that autonomy and relatedness are inseparable aspects of self-experience and necessarily exist in any culture. She argues that both within and between cultures there are complex and multifaceted relations in how these orientations are experienced. Raeff argues that many theorists have routinely characterized the European-American self in terms of autonomy and personal achievement, almost as if the self needs and desires no social relations. However, Raeff's data, gathered with in-depth interviews from

European-American adolescents, indicated many dimensions of relatedness in addition to autonomy. Her most striking findings illuminate the inseparable nature of autonomy and relatedness. As is illustrated by detailed excerpts from her interview, when adolescents were probed about the meaning of their self-descriptions many typical statements about the independent self (for instance, "I am very intellectually focused") yielded a deeply social dimension that was oriented toward social relationships. In addition to demonstrating multiplicity of self-experience, Raeff's work illustrates how cultural analysis of selfhood can occur outside of a cross-cultural design.

In Chapter Five, "The Coactive Construction of Selves in Cultures," Michael F. Mascolo builds on the research presented in this volume and elsewhere to present a *process model* describing how selves develop within and across cultures. Mascolo argues that personal, social, and cultural processes are *inseparable as causal* processes in the development of self. As such, self-awareness develops at the nexus of personal (sense of individual agency, volition, affect, and so on), social (co-regulation of action and meaning between persons), and cultural (systems of meanings distributed throughout a linguistic community) processes. As a result, although selves develop toward end points that differ dramatically with cultural groups, the experience of self in individuals from all cultures necessarily forms around an agentive and communal core.

In the final chapter, Elliot Turiel presents a commentary on the entire volume, discussing new directions and implications for further research in this area.

References

Greenfield, P. M., and Cocking, R. R. (eds.). *Cross-Cultural Roots of Minority Child Development*. Mahwah, N.J.: Erlbaum, 1994.
Hampson, S. *The Construction of Personality*. London: Routledge, 1982.
Hofstede, G. *Culture's Consequences: International Differences in Work-Related Values.* Thousand Oaks, Calif.: Sage, 1980.
Kagitçibasi, Ç. "A Critical Appraisal of Individualism and Collectivism: Toward a New Formulation." In U. Kim and others (eds.), *Individualism and Collectivism: Theory, Method, and Applications*. Thousand Oaks, Calif.: Sage, 1994.
Kim, U., and others (eds.). *Individualism and Collectivism: Theory, Method, and Applications*. Thousand Oaks, Calif.: Sage, 1994.
Markus, H. J., and Kitayama, S. "Culture and the Self: Implications for Cognition, Emotion, and Motivation." *Psychological Review*, 1991, 98(2), 224–253.
Misra, G., and Agarwal, R. "The Meaning of Achievement: Implications for a Cross-Cultural Theory of Achievement Motivation." In I. R. Lagunees and Y. H. Poortinga (eds.), *From a Different Perspective: Studies of Behavior Across Cultures*. Lisse, Netherlands: Swets and Zeitlinger, 1985.
Misra, G., and Gergen, K. J. "On the Place of Culture in Psychological Science." *International Journal of Psychology*, 1993, 28, 225–243.
Oyserman, D., Coon, H. M., and Kemmelmeier, M. "Rethinking Individualism and Collectivism: Evaluation of Theoretical Assumptions and Meta-Analyses." *Psychological Bulletin*, 2002, 128(1), 3–72.

Sampson, E. "The Deconstruction of the Self." In J. Shotter and K. Gergen (eds.), *Texts of Identity*. Thousand Oaks, Calif.: Sage, 1989.

Shweder, R. A., and Sullivan, M. A. "Cultural Psychology: Who Needs It?" *Annual Review of Psychology*, 1993, *44*, 497–523.

Sinha, D., and Tripathi, R. C. "Individualism in a Collectivist Culture: A Case of Coexistence of Opposites." In U. Kim and others (eds.), *Individualism and Collectivism: Theory, Method, and Applications*. Thousand Oaks, Calif.: Sage, 1994.

Triandis, H. C. "Theoretical and Methodological Approaches to the Study of Collectivism and Individualism." In U. Kim and others (eds.), *Individualism and Collectivism: Theory, Method, and Applications*. Thousand Oaks, Calif.: Sage, 1994.

Michael F. Mascolo
Jin Li
Editors

MICHAEL F. MASCOLO is professor of psychology at Merrimack College in North Andover, Massachusetts.

JIN LI is assistant professor of psychology at Brown University in Providence, Rhode Island.

1

A comparison involving individuals in urban areas of India and the United States reveals both individual and relational concepts of self in each sample. However, cultural differences arose in specific ways in which individual and relational concepts are constructed.

Individual and Relational Conceptions of Self in India and the United States

Michael F. Mascolo, Girishwar Misra, Christopher Rapisardi

India is sometimes described as a nation embodied by the coexistence of opposites. Sinha and Tripathi (1994) have suggested that India is a context in which individualism and collectivism coexist with each other. They suggested that, at least for India if not for other cultures, it might be helpful to think of individualism and collectivism as independent dimensions rather than as two poles of the same continuum (Kim, 1994; Triandis, 1990). As such, the comparative analysis of self in Indian and North American cultures may constitute a good launching point to examine how multiple and even divergent aspects of self coexist and co-occur within and between particular cultures. Because detailed and integrative analyses of Western conceptions of self are widely available (Bellah and others, 1985; de Tocqueville, 2001; Johnson, 1985; and Raeff's chapter in this volume), in what follows we focus upon a summary analysis of Indian conceptions of selfhood and social relations.

This work was supported and made possible by grants from Daniel and Linda Ciejek and from Merrimack College. We thank Art Ledoux for his insightful commentary on drafts of the manuscript. We also wish to acknowledge Deepa John, Sonia Machado, Kathleen Turgeon, and Lisa DiNuccio for their contributions to the study and for their assistance in collecting and analyzing data.

9

Conceptions of Self in Indian Philosophy and Culture

To understand the complexity of Indian conceptions of selfhood, it is necessary to turn to an analysis of Indian philosophy and religion. Indian philosophy, with its rich emphasis on spiritual interiority and social duty, penetrates Indian values and consciousness to this very day (Bharati, 1985; Saskena, 1967b). Of course, any attempt to analyze Indian philosophy, religion, and culture must come to grips with the extraordinary diversity that characterizes Indian history, thought, and culture. There are many philosophical and religious traditions in India. In this section, we merely summarize some common threads that run through much traditional Indian philosophy as it pertains to selfhood and social life.

The Spiritual Interiority of Indian Selfhood. Figure 1.1 summarizes a representation of traditional Indian (Hindi/Buddhist) philosophy of selfhood. The Indian conception of the individual (*jīvātman*) is depicted at point *a*. Indian philosophy depicts the individual as a series of five sheaths or *kośa* (Bharati, 1985). The four inner sheaths are material in that they are composed of matter. The successive sheaths include the body; the senses; the mind, thinking organ (*manas*), or "ego" (*ahamkāra*); intellect or reflection (*buddhi*); and finally the *ātman*. Although Indian philosophy speaks of body, senses, mind, and intellect, none of these material entities or processes is regarded as the *self*. The self consists of *ātman*, which is a purely and deeply spiritual entity or process. The *ātman* is the realization of one's true or essential self, and the realization that one's essential self is indistinguishable from absolute reality, which is known as *Brahman*. *Brahman* consists of the spiritual absolute, which is not only ubiquitous but also free of both form and matter.

At the beginning of life, the Indian *ātman* is "fused" with the material elements of the individual. The realization of *ātman* must therefore be attained through a lifelong and effortful process. Pathways to *ātman* are depicted at point *b* in Figure 1.1. Traditional Hindu philosophy articulates four stages of life (*ārama*), the last stage of which affords the possibility of attaining *ātman* and the corresponding state of spiritual emancipation known as *moksa* (Kakar, 1979; Mahadevan, 1967). In the first stage, individuals assume the tasks of studentship and discipline (*brahmacarya*). The student lives in the house of his teacher and receives instruction in science and art. In the next stage, a person gets married, has children, and assumes the role and responsibilities of householder (*gārhastha*). Traditional marriages are arranged, not simply a marriage of individuals but more fundamentally of families. The marriage begins a process where spouses enjoin in a process of righteous living. As the (male) individual begins to age, there begins a process of separation from the family and his responsibilities to family and society. Traditionally, the Hindu individual may go to live in the forest and begin a directed and ascetic life seeking spiritual enlightenment. The last stage consists of full renunciation of society (*sannyāsa*). During this

Figure 1.1. Indian Conception of Selfhood

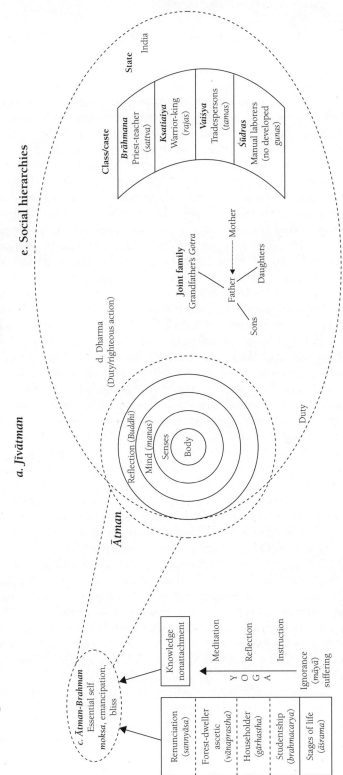

last stage, the individual renounces worldly concerns and spends his time in contemplation, seeking perfection in the supreme goal of *moksa* (spiritual emancipation, freedom). This final goal state is depicted in Figure 1.1 at point *c*.

An understanding of *moksa* and *ātman* is facilitated through a further analysis of yoga as a pathway to perfection in traditional Indian philosophy (Mahadevan, 1967; Nikhilananda, 1967). In Indian philosophy, the term *yoga* means "yoking," "union," or uniting with an ultimate reality. A basic state of human condition involves *suffering*, which, in Buddhist philosophy, has its origin in ignorance (*māyā*). Ignorance is dispelled through knowledge, which is attained through concentration. Yoga consists of a series of practices to concentrate and restrain the mind in order to learn the basic truths of internal and external life. A result of restraining the mind is nonattachment. Through concentration, one controls the yearning for any desired object, material or immaterial, in one's life. The nonattached person renounces attachment for anything in the natural (material) world, including the mind. In a state of nonattachment, the person becomes a witness to his or her mind and can observe its processes without attachment to it. Successful nonattachment ultimately results in a state of spiritual liberation from the material and an awareness of the true nature of self (Saskena, 1967a). This results in *moksa* (freedom, bliss) and an awareness of the lack of distinction between self and nonself, between *ātman* and *Brahman*. In the state of *moksa*, there is an awareness that *ātman* equals *Brahman* (absolute spiritual reality). In some forms of Buddhism, as *ātman* fuses with *Brahman* one's true, essential self is understood as *no-self* or *anatta* (Bharati, 1985).

Duty and Hierarchy in Indian Social Selves. Whereas Indian philosophy ultimately unites an inner self to a transcendent spiritual reality, Indian social and moral philosophy binds selves to social relations. Indian philosophy postulates four social values. In order of importance, they are *moksa* (spiritual emancipation), *dharma* (righteous action), *artha* (wealth), and *kāma* (pleasure). As indicated earlier in this discussion, spiritual values (*moksa*) are most important. However, *artha* and *kāma* are also important; "[m]an [sic] has to live before he can live spiritually" (Mahadevan, 1967, p. 154). This requires a certain degree of wealth and fulfillment of bodily desires. Nonetheless, spiritual and moral values prevail and structure social life. In this regard, the concept of *dharma* is essential (point *d* in Figure 1.1). *Dharma* consists of righteous action and adherence to a natural and moral order. In this way, dharma is both a sociomoral principle and an expression of each person's inner nature. The basic rule of *dharma* is to *perform the duties that pertain to one's station in life* (Mahadevan, 1967). This is the foundation of the Indian morality of *duty* (Miller, 1994).

Miller (1994) offers a compelling analysis of the duty morality in traditional Hindu society. According to Miller, in contrast to Western conceptions of morality, which are organized around concepts such as individual rights and care, traditional Hindu morality is organized around the concept of duty. Within Western moral systems (Kant, 1989; Kohlberg, 1984; Rawls, 1971), moral systems are organized around the liberal ideal of freedom. From this view, human individuals are fundamentally free to act, so long as their actions do not impinge upon the liberties and rights of others. Thus, in Western moral systems, beyond the requirement to refrain from actions that impinge upon others' liberties, an individual has no moral obligations toward others (for example, to help another person in need). In contrast, the Hindu concept of duty (*dharma*) specifies systems of supererogatory obligations, involving self-sacrifice (Mascolo and Bhatia, 2002; Miller, 1994), that occur within relationships. Social responsibilities toward the other are mandatory rather than optional. These responsibilities follow from an individual's *dharma*, the inner moral nature whose cultivation binds him or her to righteous action and to obligations to other people within a social hierarchy.

Within Indian philosophy and culture, a person is born into a system of duties and relationships defined by the hierarchical nature of Indian society. They include duties defined by one's position in one's (1) extended family, (2) class or caste (*jāti*), and (3) state (India itself). These duties are represented at point *f* in Figure 1.1. One's primary duties are to the extended family. The joint family is defined in terms of male members descended lineally from a common male ancestor, along with their respective wives, sons, and daughters. The extended family is hierarchically structured by kinship position and gender. When a woman marries, she leaves her family to become a part of her husband's extended family (*gotra*). Within this system, one shows *deference, loyalty and subordination* to superiors; in turn, one expects *nurturance, concern, care, and responsibility* from superiors. For example, a father is regarded as hierarchically superior to his children but will always be subordinate to his father throughout life. Indian culture preserves hierarchies among brothers by birth order viewed in relation to their father, but as equals when viewed in relation to their mother. A wife is subordinate to her husband and all older brothers, but she may maintain a more informal relationship to younger brothers (Chand, 1967; Roland, 1988).

An Analysis of Indian and North American Selves-in-Relationships

We next report the results of a study comparing representations of self-in-relationships from samples of urban-dwelling individuals from India and the United States. In so doing, we examined how individual and communal concerns were represented in the experience of self-in-relationships from individuals in both samples. In so doing, we did not simply attempt to differentiate Indian and American samples in terms of individualist and collectivist themes, but also to represent specific differences in how individuality and social connectedness were constructed in both samples.

Procedure. Thirty-eight women and men between the ages of fourteen and sixty-seven participated, half from the greater Boston, Massachusetts, area (mean age thirty-two years) and half from urban Delhi, India (mean age thirty years). The sample was predominantly female. There were five participants below the age of eighteen in each sample (mean age sixteen years for both samples). Both samples were predominantly female (eighteen females and one male for Boston, fourteen females and five males for Delhi). Both samples were primarily Christian (fourteen Christian and five unspecified for Boston; eleven Christian, five Hindu, one Muslim, and two unspecified for Delhi). The sample was drawn from a primarily middle-class population. Because of the relatively low number of adolescents in the study, all analyses were performed collapsed across age.

All interviews were conducted in English. Participants completed an adaptation of Harter and Monsour's *self-in-relationships* interview (1992). Participants were asked to indicate positive and negative ways in which they "acted and experienced themselves" when they were with each of nine role figures: their mother, father, sibling, a friend, superordinate, subordinate, child, a romantic partner, and "when you are just being the 'real you.'" They were asked to provide at least three descriptions of self for each role figure. Interviewers used the clinical method to clarify the meaning of these descriptions to each individual.

Self-descriptions were recorded, using the subject's own words, onto gummed labels. Participants were given a "self-portrait" that consisted of three concentric circles. The innermost circle was reserved for the self-descriptions that were seen as "most important" to the participant; the next layer was for "less important" attributes, and the outer rung for attributes viewed as "least important." Participants were asked to affix the gummed labels upon the "self-portrait" according to how the participant felt the attributes went together.

A Structural Representation of Self-in-Relationships. To develop a scheme for categorizing the self-descriptions, we pored over the interviews several times in order to develop a sense of the structural similarities and differences in the self-descriptions. Informed by Damon and Hart's multidimensional model of self (1988), we differentiated four *relational orientations* defined in terms of the direction of the action between self and other. *Within-self descriptions* consist of descriptions of action and experience that occur within the self and that are not directed at another person (for example, "I feel calm"). Descriptions involving *mutuality* consist of shared or reciprocal actions and experience that occur jointly between persons ("we love each other"). Descriptions of *other-relating-to-self* refer to representations of the actions and experiences of other people that are about or directed toward the self ("she loves me"); conversely, descriptions of *self-relating-to-other* represent action and experiences in the self that are about or directed toward others ("I love him").

In addition to the four relational orientations, we were able to discriminate six *domains of self-in-relational experience. Emotions and feelings* include reports of felt experiences and bodily states indicated by terms of emotion or state (such as "angry," "jealous"); *evaluations* include explicit

Table 1.1. A Structural Representation of Self-Experience

Relational Orientation; Facets of Self-in-Relation	Within-Self (references to aspects of self that can be experienced within the individual or by self alone)	Mutuality (descriptions of reciprocal ways that self and other relate or are connected to each other)	Other-to-Self (descriptions of how the other relates to or experiences the self)	Self-to-Other (descriptions of how the self relates to or experiences the other)
Emotions and Feelings: references to felt experience and bodily states	Inner emotion: feelings or bodily states experienced within the self or without the other; "happy," "calm," "hyper"	Mutual feeling: references to reciprocal or mutual ways of feeling between self and other; "we love each other"	O's feelings toward S: feelings (emotion terms) that other has toward self; "loves me"	S's feelings toward O: feelings (emotion terms) that self has toward other; "love her"
Evaluation: explicit assessments of positive or negative value of target events	Self-evaluations: evaluations of the self by the self; "insecure," "confident"	Mutual evaluations: mutual, or reciprocal evaluations that occur between persons; "we respect each other"	O's evaluation of self: evaluations of the self by the other; "has confidence in me"	Relational self-evaluations: comparative evaluations (e.g., "superior"); self-evaluations defined in terms of others (e.g., "proud with him")
Interactive mode: references to ways of relating or communicating to another person	Private time: references to absence of or negation of interaction or communication; "moments of quiet reflection"	Reciprocal communication: references to reciprocal ways of relating between people; "we have open communication"	O's role in interaction: how other relates to, acts toward, or communicates with the self; "listens to me"	S's role in interaction: how self relates, acts toward, or communicates with other; "friendly," "stern"
Intimacy: references to ways of being connected with or close to others	Relating to the self: ways of caring for or forming a relationship with the self; "need time to be with myself"	Mutuality in relationship: quality or nature of affective relationship between persons; "we are there for each other"	O's role in relationship: how other cares for or is connected to the self; "cares about me"	S's role in relationship: how self cares for or is connected to the other; "connected to her"
Dependency: references to ways of relying upon other persons	Independence: how self functions without help of others; "independent"	Interdependence: how self and other rely upon each other; "we depend on each other"	S depends on O: how self relies on other; "protected by"	O depends on S: how other relies on self; "protective of"
Roles and dispositions: references to stable behavior patterns, social roles, or identifications	Personal attributes and agency: personal attributes, identities, or powers of agency; "athlete," "responsible"	Reciprocal social roles and dispositions: how social role or identities of self and other are related to each other; "I'm the mother; she's the child"	O's social role/disposition relative to S: other's social role, identity, and traits in relation to self; "father to me"	S's social role/disposition relative to O: self's social role, identity, and traits in relation to self; "I'm the boss"

Table 1.2. Number and Proportion of Self-Descriptions by Nation and Relational Orientation

Relational Orientation	Boston	Delhi
Within self	.23	.18*
Mutuality	.14	.06***
Other to self	.12	.18**
Self to other	.51	.59*

Note: * = .05; ** = .01; *** = .001.
Boldface indicates significant findings.

assessments of the positive or negative value of aspects of self, other, and so on ("I like myself"). *Modes of interacting and communicating* include references to how individuals relate, act, or communicate in interactions with others ("kind," "talkative"). *Modes of intimacy* include references to ways of being close or connected within interpersonal relationships ("loving toward him," "secure with her"). *Dependency relations* include statements of how social partners rely upon, protect, give aid to, or support one another ("protective," "watch over her"). Finally, *roles, identities, and dispositions* index stable social roles, identities, and dispositions of self or social partners ("responsible," "hard working," "athlete"). These two broad dimensions yielded a six-by-four *experience domain by relational orientation* matrix (Table 1.1).

Table 1.2 contains a comparative analysis of the mean number of self-descriptions produced for each relational orientation by nation. American participants produced more within-self and mutual self-descriptions, whereas Indian participants produced more self-relating-to-other and other-relating-to-self descriptions. (All reports of statistical significance were conducted using chi square analyses.) In both the American and Indian samples, the largest proportion of total self-descriptions consists of self-to-other attributes (.51 and .59 respectively). Whereas other-to-self descriptions occupied the smallest proportion of descriptions for the American sample (.14), descriptions of mutuality were least frequent among Indian participants (.06).

The finding that American participants described themselves more often with within-self attributes and that Indian participants describe themselves more often with relational attributes is consistent with an I-C discrimination between U.S. and Indian culture. However, within-self descriptions were by no means absent from Indian self-descriptions. Further, self-to-other descriptions occupied the majority of self-attributes for both Indian and American samples. Initially, on the premise that members of more collectivist societies would fashion more interdependent "we-self" identities (Marcus and Kitayama, 1991; Roland, 1988), we expected greater mutuality among Indian than American participants. The finding of

**Table 1.3. Mean Number and Proportion of Self-Descriptions by
Type of Self-Facet and Nation**

Facet of Self-in-Relation	Boston	Delhi
Emotions	.16	.14
Evaluations	**.13**	**.08***
Communication	.24	**.30***
Intimacy	.22	.23
Dependency	.09	.11
Role/disposition	.15	.13

Note: * = .05.

Boldface indicates significant findings.

greater mutuality among U.S. participants reflects a definition of mutuality in terms of egalitarian relations. With exceptions, participants in the American sample described mutuality primarily in terms of reciprocity among separable equals ("We love each other," "We are there for each other," "We get along well together").

Table 1.3 contains a comparison of the mean number of self-descriptions produced for each domain of self-experience as a function of nation. As indicated, a similar mean number of self-descriptions and proportion of total self-descriptions were produced in the American and Indian samples for emotions; modes of intimacy; modes of dependency; and roles, identities, and dispositions. There was a small tendency for participants from the United States to produce more evaluations than Indian participants, and for Indian participants to produce more descriptions of modes of communication.

These results suggest that the Indian and American participants make similar distinctions in the broad types of self-facets that they experience in relation to others. However, as indicated in Table 1.2, Indian and American participants differed in the relational orientations within which self-facets were framed. Against the backdrop of broad similarity, there was a bias in favor of within-self and mutual orientations for the U.S. sample, and relational orientations for the Indian sample.

Cultural Meanings of Self-in-Relation. Here we examine the specific meanings of self-descriptions constructed by Indian and American participants within each relational orientation that has been described.

Within-Self Descriptions. Table 1.4 depicts the proportion of within-self descriptions categorized into a series of within-self subclasses by culture. For emotions and feelings, both Indian and American participants reported a similar degree of positive affect (for example, "happy," "enjoy life"). However, American participants reported more negative affect ("nervous," "sad," and so on) and calm-excited affect ("invigorated," "calm," "hyper") than did Indian participants. This latter finding is corroborated with the

Table 1.4. Mean Number of Individual Within-Individual Self-Descriptions by Nation

Within-Self Attributes	Boston	Delhi
Emotions:		
Positive affect	.14	.14
Negative affect	**.08**	.02*
Calm-excited	**.08**	.00*
Self-evaluations:		
Positive	.17	.14
Negative	.09	.05
Communicative	.01	.01
Intimacy	.00	.01
Dependency	.00	.02
Roles/disposition:		
Easygoing-energetic	**.13**	.03**
Myself/free to be me	**.09**	.02**
Free	.00	**.14***
Spiritual/religious	.01	**.06***
Professional achievement	.02	.08
Individual agency	.09	.16

Note: * = .05; ** = .01.
Boldface indicates significant findings.

results of the analysis roles, identities, and dispositions. American participants more often (almost once per participant) reported dispositions along
a relaxed-energetic dimension ("carefree," "easygoing," "relaxed," "unsta-
ble," "energetic") than did Indian participants.

Similarly, Americans more often reported a sense of being "myself" or
of being "free to be myself" than did Indians; conversely, Indians were more
likely to report feelings of being simply "free." Indians reported being religious or spiritual to a greater degree than Americans. Interestingly, participants from both nations described themselves in terms of professional
achievement (for example, hard-working, goal-oriented, always learning at
work) and individual agency ("creative," "imaginative," "[in]decisive,"
"[ir]responsible") at similar levels.

Descriptions of Mutuality. Table 1.5 depicts the proportion of mutuality descriptions categorized into a series of subclasses by culture. Indians
and American participants described themselves in terms of mutual affec-
tion (for example, "We love each other") and mutual positive evaluation
("We respect each other") at similar, albeit low, levels of responding.
However, Indians and Americans differed in their descriptions of mutual
intimacy. Americans described intimacy much more often in terms of
mutual closeness ("very close despite distance"; "we're close"; "we remain

Table 1.5. Mutuality in Self-Experience by Nation

Descriptions of Mutuality (S ↔ O)	Boston	Delhi
Emotion:		
Love other	.09	.09
Evaluation:		
Mutual positive	.08	.03
Modes of interaction:		
Reciprocal communication	**.24**	.09***
Intimacy:		
Mutual closeness	**.34**	.09***
Mutual friends	**.08**	.00*
"We" feeling; sharing	.01	**.33****
Dependency:		
Interdependent	.03	.00
Role/disposition:		
Equality	.00	.09
Reciprocal roles	.05	.03

Note: * = .05; ** = .01; *** = .001.
Boldface indicates significant findings.

very connected") and mutual friendship ("we're friends"); Indian respondents describe their intimate relations more often than American participants in terms of what might be called a *we* feeling ("we feeling," "sharing," "togetherness"). Interestingly, few participants from either sample described relations in terms of interdependence.

Other-in-Relation-to-Self. Descriptions of how individuals experience others relating to the self indicated dramatic effects. Table 1.6 depicts the proportion of other-to-self descriptions put into subclasses by culture. Although American participants described themselves more often as receiving esteem or respect ("respected," "well-liked," "admired"), Indian participants described themselves as feeling cared for and loved ("cared for," "loved," "lovable," "wanted") to a far greater extent than American participants did.

In addition, although Americans and Indians described themselves as helped or supported with similar frequency, Indians reported being protected or dependent on others to a greater degree than did Americans. Descriptions that were classified as helped or supported consisted of those implying that the self is primarily responsible for a task, and that others provide secondary assistance to the self (helped, assisted, and so on). Descriptions categorized as protected (such as "protected," "dependent [on other]," "she takes care of me") highlight the responsibility of the other to watch over or guide the self from harm.

Table 1.6. Sense of Other-in-Relation-to-Self by Nation

Other Relating to Self (S ← O)	Boston	Delhi
Emotions:		
Loved	.14	**.19***
Evaluations:		
Receive respect/esteem	**.17**	**.03***
Receive negative evaluation	.00	.00
Communication:		
Other dominates me	.05	**.12****
Other sensitive to me	.10	.05
Intimacy:		
Cared for	.22	**.38****
Trusted	.03	.01
Dependency:		
Protected by/dependent on other	.05	**.09***
Supported	.14	.10
Role/disposition	.12	.02

Note: * = .05; ** = .01.
Boldface indicates significant findings.

Finally, whereas American and Indian participants described others as sensitive ("he is sensitive," "listens to me") to the self with equal frequency, to a greater extent than Americans Indian participants described others as dominating ("dominated," "suffocated," "abused," "pressured").

Self-in-Relation-to-Other. The largest proportion of self-descriptions fell into the self-to-other orientation. As indicated in Table 1.7, with regard to emotions, although American and Indian participants described themselves as enjoying (for instance, "have fun with," "enjoy") or nervous with others ("nervous," "afraid to mess up," "anxious with," "worry about") at a similar frequency, Americans were more likely than Indians to describe feelings of love (such as "love him") toward other. Conversely, Indians were more likely than Americans to report feelings of anger ("angry," "frustrated," "annoyed"), jealousy ("jealous," "envious"), and social pride (proud of the self when with the other person) in relation to others. Regarding modes of interaction, Indians and Americans described themselves as sensitive ("sensitive," "listening") and open ("open," "open to his suggestions") with others with similar frequency. However, Indian participants described themselves as friendly ("friendly," "kind," "jovial," "cheerful") more often than Americans did.

An important set of findings concerned representation of self around issues related to authority. To a much greater degree than Americans, Indian respondents described themselves as respectful or obedient. This finding was dramatic: Indians reported respectful or obedient behavior

Table 1.7. Sense of Self-in-Relation-to-Other by Nation

Self Relating to Other (S → O)	Boston	Delhi
Emotions:		
Love other	.02	.00*
Angry with other	.03	**.05***
Fearful/anxious	.03	.03
Enjoy	.04	.02
Empathy	.00	.00
Jealous/envy of other	.00	.02*
Evaluations:		
Proud of self with other	.02	**.04***
Negative self-evaluation with other	.00	.01
Respect other	.02	.00
General positive evaluation	.04	.02
Modes of interaction:		
Friendly	.05	**.10*****
Open	.07	.08
Sensitive/listening	.07	.06
Respectful/obedient	.00	**.06*****
Domineering/authoritative	.02	**.05***
Resist authority	**.03**	.00*
Introverted	.03	.04
Extroverted	**.07**	.02*
Intimacy:		
Loving, caring, concerned for	.18	.19
Honest, sincere	.06	.02
Dependency:		
Protective/responsible for	.02	**.05****
Nurture other	.02	.00
Helpful/support/assist/advise	.09	.06
Role/identity:		
Hierarchy (boss-worker; parent-child)	.02	.01
Social trait (e.g., funny; feministic)	.02	.01
Social agency	.02	.00

Note: * = .05; ** = .01; *** = .001.
Boldface indicates significant findings.

toward others at least once per interview, but this theme was virtually absent for American participants. In this regard, although Indians described themselves as "respectful" and "well-mannered" (terms that commonly earn approbation in the West), they also invoked terms such as "obedient" and "surrendering" (terms that are much more likely to have a negative connotation in the West). In addition, to a greater extent than Americans, Indian participants invoked a domineering or authoritative dimension to describe themselves (for example, "domineering," "stern," "strict," "imposing," "not bossy") in relation to others. By contrast, American participants more often described themselves as resisting authority ("know when to hold my ground") than did Indian participants. Further, although Americans and Indians viewed themselves with equal frequency as introverts (introverted, reserved, "quiet around him"), Americans were much more likely than Indians to view themselves as extroverts ("extroverted," "talkative," "outgoing"). This finding may reflect the shared value of inhibiting rather than expressing the self to others in India, especially within hierarchical relations.

Finally, descriptions of being loving or caring ("loving," caring," "concerned for," "close," "secure," "attached") were the most frequently produced attributes in either sample. Whereas both Indian and American participants described themselves as supportive ("help her," "guiding," "support him") and nurturing ("I would mother them," "need to take care of her"), Indians more frequently described themselves as protective of others ("protective," "responsible for"). Again, to protect or be responsible for communicates a greater degree of active obligation toward the other than do concepts such as supporting, helping, or assisting.

Multiplicity of Selfhood Within and Between Cultures

As indicated in Table 1.1, the representation and experience of self is complex and multifaceted in both urban U.S. and Indian samples. Participants from both samples were able to represent self in terms of inner and individual experiences as well as in terms of mutuality and various relations between self and other. As such, Table 1.1 presents a system of etic categories that allow cross-cultural comparisons of self-experience. Consistent with research in the I-C tradition, within the context of broad cultural similarities Americans produced more self-descriptions involving inner experience and mutuality, whereas Indians produced more self-to-other and other-to-self representations. Tables 4 through 7 describe more localized (emic) meanings of these dimensions of self. Results suggest how differences in local meanings contextualize broad etic dimensions.

Indian and American cultural histories embody traditions that draw upon agentic and communal values, albeit in very different forms. Indian philosophical systems embrace both deep inner spirituality and duty-based sociomoral obligations. Indian conceptions of spiritual interiority are central organizers of duty-based morality. Through devotional practices involving meditation, yoga, and righteous action (*dharma*), one's ultimate individual goal is to cultivate the awareness that one's essential self (*ātman*) is indistinguishable from transcendent reality (*Brahman*). Thus an individual's interior (and even solitary) spiritual path is quintessentially connected to the larger spiritual order, in much the same way as the self's functions in everyday life are directed toward fulfilling one's rightful place in a hierarchical social order.

Figure 1.2 depicts four conceptions of selfhood that can exist between and within cultures. Representations of independent and interdependent selves draw upon the work of Marcus and Kitayama (1991), who proposed that people from individualist cultures construct predominantly independent self-conceptions. Within the independent view, they are viewed as separate and distinct from each other; social relations are based upon choice and social contract. Those authors suggest that in more collectivist societies people define the self in terms of relationships to others and to social groups. From this view, people construct a more interdependent sense of self. In this model, the distinction between self and other is blurred; the boundaries of the self are permeable and open to the influence of others.

In the present study, individual conceptions of self were represented in the responses of participants from the U.S. and Indian samples in the form of positive and negative affect and self-evaluation, a sense of agency and ambition. For Americans, independent representations also centered on the freedom "to be me"; Indians were more likely to represent the self as simply "free." For Americans, "free to be me" implies the freedom to express the self, to act naturally without regard for expectations of others. For Indian participants, free implied freedom from social constraints, but this freedom also enables more active engagement with others. For example, one Indian female suggested that feeling private and feeling free were opposite experiences: "Private means keeping a part of you to yourself while free means sharing, interacting, etc." Although individuals from both samples use the term *free,* the American definition is organized around unencumbered self-expression, whereas the Indian conception suggests the ability to pursue social engagement without constraint.

For Americans, interdependent representations centered on mutual and reciprocal relations between self and other viewed as equals (as in "we're there for each other"). For Indians, when interdependent representations of self were provided, they were more likely to reflect a sense of shared experience with the other. As such, although interdependent representations of self were represented in both samples, interdependence among American participants was organized around what Roland (1988) called an "I-self"; Indians organize interdependence to a greater degree than Americans around what Roland calls the "we-self."

One might suggest that the relational self constitutes a third way of conceiving the self-in-relation-to-others (see Fogel, 1993; Gergen, 1987; Hermans, Kempen, and van Loon, 1992; Mascolo and Fischer, 1998). Instead of viewing selves as either separate from or merged with others, one might define the self in terms of dispositions and actions in dialogical relation with others. From this view, although selves are distinct from each other, they are not independent of each other. When a person is open, friendly, or hostile to another (that is, a self-to-other disposition) or feels "listened to," "cared for," or "hated" by another (other-to-self disposition),

Figure 1.2. Four Models of Self-in-Relationship

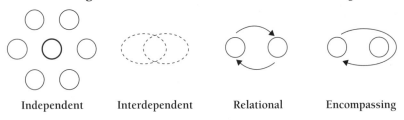

Independent   Interdependent   Relational   Encompassing

there is a clear sense that the self and other are different (distinct). However, self and other act with reference to each other; neither is independent of the other's functioning. Moreover, such self-to-other or other-to-self relations display many types of symmetry and asymmetry. The proclivity for Indian participants to represent the self in terms of self-to-other and other-to-self modes is consistent with the Indian sociomoral value of *dharma* (righteous duty).

A final model consists of an encompassing sense of self. We use the term *encompassing* to refer to a sense of the self being subsumed by the other or otherwise embedded in a relationship that extends beyond the self alone. We suggest that an encompassing sense of self arises in relationships where one person is obligated to, is responsible for, or views himself or herself as the caretaker of the other. Self-experience of this sort is likely to be well represented in hierarchical relationships, which are more salient in India than in the United States. For example, in Indian social life such hierarchical identifications occur within parent-child, superior-subordinate, and husband-wife (and even sibling) relationships. Note here that within such relationships neither person is passive. Both the superior and the subordinate have moral duties in relation to each other, even if those duties exhibit hierarchical asymmetry. Where a father, mother, superior, or brother may be responsible for protecting a child, subordinate, or sibling, the latter individual plays a role in actively respecting, obeying, and appreciating the sacrifice and care provided by the other. Note that an encompassing sense of self does not necessarily imply a blurring of boundaries between self and other. One person may know what is expected of him or her even if this duty is experienced as burdensome or sacrificial (Mascolo and Bhatia, 2002). In this way, the sacrificing person is aware that her sacrifice reflects her *own* suffering. Her act is performed out of duty within the relationship, but also in the context of the positive experiences she adduces from being part of that relationship. An encompassing self may be more prevalent among Indians, but Americans can experience an encompassing self in relationship with children or mentors.

Thus, in analyzing conceptions of self within cultures, we would argue the importance of local uniqueness amid broad commonality. No single conception of self exists either within or between cultures. As such, although the models of self indicated in Figure 1.2 are represented in some form in virtually all cultures, some models are more dominant than others. In the United States, self-conceptions are organized around individualist and relational representations; in urban Delhi, relational and encompassing models are primary. As such, in any given culture multiple conceptions of self are organized with reference to such dominant cultural meanings.

References

Bellah, R. N., and others. *Habits of the Heart: Individualism and Commitment in American Life.* Berkeley: University of California Press, 1985.

Bharati, A. "The Self in Hindu Thought and Action." In G. Marsella, A. J. DeVos, and F.L.K. Hsu (eds.), *Culture and Self.* New York: Tavistock, 1985.

Chand, T. "The Individual in the Legal and Political Thought and Institutions of India." In C. A. Moore (ed.), *The Indian Mind: Essentials of Indian Philosophy and Culture.* Honolulu: East-West Center Press/University of Hawaii Press, 1967.

Damon, W., and Hart, D. *Self-Understanding in Childhood and Adolescence.* Cambridge: Cambridge University Press, 1988.

De Tocqueville, A. *Democracy in America.* New York: Signet, 2001. (Originally published 1835)

Emerson, R. W. *Self-Reliance and Other Essays.* New York: Dover, 1993. (Originally published 1841)

Etzioni, A. *The Spirit of Community: The Reinvention of American Society.* New York: Simon & Schuster, 1994.

Fogel, A. *Developing Through Relationships: Origins of Communication, Self, and Culture.* Chicago: University of Chicago Press, 1993.

Gergen, K. J. "Toward Self as Relationship." In T. Honness and K. Yardley (eds.), *Self and Identity: Psychosocial Perspectives.* New York: Wiley, 1987.

Harter, S., and Monsour, A. "Developmental Analysis of Conflict Caused by Opposing Attributes in the Adolescent Self-Portrait." *Developmental Psychology,* 1992, *28*(2), 251–260.

Hermans, H.J.M., Kempen, H.J.G., and van Loon, R.J.P. "The Dialogical Self: Beyond Individualism and Rationalism." *American Psychologist,* 1992, *47,* 23–33.

Johnson, F. "The Western Concept of Self." In G. Marsella, A. J. DeVos, and F.L.K. Hsu (eds.), *Culture and Self.* New York: Tavistock, 1985.

Kagitçibasi, Ç. "A Critical Appraisal of Individualism and Collectivism: Toward a New Formulation." In U. Kim and others (eds.), *Individualism and Collectivism: Theory, Method, and Applications.* Thousand Oaks, Calif.: Sage, 1994.

Kakar, S. *Identity and Adulthood.* Delhi, India: Oxford University Press, 1979.

Kant, I. *The Foundations of the Metaphysics of Morals.* Upper Saddle River, N.J.: Prentice Hall, 1989. (Originally published 1785)

Kim, U. "Individualism and Collectivism: Conceptual Clarification and Elaboration." In U. Kim and others (eds.), *Individualism and Collectivism: Theory, Method, and Applications.* Thousand Oaks, Calif.: Sage, 1994.

Kohlberg, L. *The Philosophy of Moral Development: Moral Stages and the Idea of Justice.* New York: HarperCollins, 1984.

Mahadevan, T.M.P. "Social, Ethical and Spiritual Values in Indian Philosophy." In C. A. Moore (ed.), *The Indian Mind: Essentials of Indian Philosophy and Culture.* Honolulu: East-West Center Press/University of Hawaii Press, 1967.

Marcus, H., and Kitayama, S. "Culture and the Self: Implications for Cognition, Emotion, and Motivation." *Psychological Review,* 1991, *98,* 225–253.

Mascolo, M. F., and Bhatia, S. "The Dynamic Construction of Culture, Self and Social Relations." *Culture and Developing Societies,* 2002, *14,* 55–92.

Mascolo, M. F., and Fischer, K. W. "The Development of Self Through the Coordination of Component Systems." In M. Ferrari and R. Sternberg (eds.), *Self-Awareness: Its Nature and Development.* New York: Guilford, 1998.

Mill, J. S. *On Liberty.* (4th ed.) London: Longman, Green, Longman, Roberts & Green, 1959.

Miller, J. "Cultural Diversity in the Morality of Caring: Individually-Oriented Versus Duty-Based Interpersonal Moral Codes." *Cross-Cultural Research,* 1994, 28(1), 3–39.

Nikhilananda, S. "Concentration and Mediation as Methods in Indian Philosophy." In C. A. Moore (ed.), *The Indian Mind: Essentials of Indian Philosophy and Culture.* Honolulu: East-West Center Press/University of Hawaii Press, 1967.

Rawls, J. *A Theory of Justice.* Cambridge, Mass.: Harvard University Press, 1971.

Rogow, A. A. *A Fatal Friendship: Alexander Hamilton and Aaron Burr.* New York: Basic Books, 1999.

Roland, A. *In Search of Self in India and Japan.* Princeton, N.J.: Princeton University Press, 1988.

Ruggero, E. *Duty First: West Point and the Making of American Leaders.* New York: HarperCollins, 2001.

Saskena, S. K. "The Individual in Social Thought and Practice in India." In C. A. Moore (ed.), *The Indian Mind: Essentials of Indian Philosophy and Culture.* Honolulu: East-West Center Press/University of Hawaii Press, 1967a.

Saskena, S. K. "Relation of Philosophical Theories to the Practical Affairs of Men." In C. A. Moore (ed.), *The Indian Mind: Essentials of Indian Philosophy and Culture.* Honolulu: East-West Center Press/University of Hawaii Press, 1967b.

Sinha, D., and Tripathi, R. C. "Individualism in a Collectivist Culture: A Case of Coexistence of Opposites." In U. Kim and others (eds.), *Individualism and Collectivism: Theory, Method, and Applications.* Thousand Oaks, Calif.: Sage, 1994.

Triandis, H. C. "Cross-Cultural Studies of Individualism and Collectivism." In J. J. Berman (ed.), *Cross-Cultural Perspectives, Nebraska Symposium on Motivation.* Lincoln: University of Nebraska Press, 1990.

Williams, J. K. *Dueling in the Old South: Vignettes of Social History.* College Station: Texas A&M Press, 1984.

MICHAEL F. MASCOLO is professor of psychology at Merrimack College in North Andover, Massachusetts.

GIRISHWAR MISRA is professor of psychology at the University of Delhi, India.

CHRISTOPHER RAPISARDI is a graduate student in psychology at the University of New Haven, Connecticut.

2

We present our recent research on children's learning goals and personal agency in the domain of learning in order to show the complexity of selves in Chinese culture. Our research poses challenges to the widely claimed collectivist self-concept in Chinese children and calls for reexamination of selves in specific domains across cultures.

Self in Learning Among Chinese Children

Jin Li, Xiaodong Yue

One's self-orientation is an important outcome of growing up in one's culture. Individualist versus collectivist (I-C) selves have been argued and observed to exist as the two basic types of selves in the world that correspond to the two cultural orientations of I-C (Hofstede, 1980; Triandis, 1995). Individualist selves are said to be bounded, autonomous, distinct from others, and emphasizing one's own goals and agency rather than those of others. By contrast, collectivist selves are connected and interdependent, stressing roles and relationships more than individual uniqueness; they are principally motivated to pursue group goals rather than their own. Therefore their sense of agency is also socially defined.

The Collectivist Chinese Self

This research tradition characterizes Chinese culture as typically collectivist (Hostede, 1980). Chinese selves, accordingly, are also collectivist (Bond and Forgas, 1984; Leung and Bond, 1984; Triandis, McCusker, and Hui, 1990). Two sources of support are compelling. First, researchers in this area typically evoke Confucianism, the dominant social thought that has been influencing Chinese lives throughout history. Maintaining social harmony as expressed in one's social position (role) is indeed one of the essential life tasks espoused by Confucianism (Hsu, 1981; K. S. Yang, 1997). Important social practices such as filial piety, friendship, and superior-subordinate relationships all center around social harmony. Compared to this well-established sociocentric system, the notion of the individual does appear to be downplayed (Ho, 1986).

In addition to Confucianism, empirical research has produced consistent findings that Chinese selves are primarily socially oriented. For example, Leung and Bond (1984) found that Chinese showed a higher concern for in-group harmony in their reward allocation than their American counterparts. Similarly, Chinese scored higher on their belief in groups and feelings of interpersonal concerns than Americans (Hui and Triandis, 1986). They also gave more social responses when defining the self and perceived themselves much closer to their in-groups than to out-groups (Triandis, McCusker, and Hui, 1990). Recent research on Chinese autobiographical memory also documents the Chinese self as more connected to social activities (Wang, 2001). Finally, Chinese were found to attribute more group than individual agency to causality than did Westerners (Menon, Morris, Chiu, and Hong, 1999).

Countering Claims

It is clear that the Chinese self as a whole is more socially than individually delineated and developed. However, inquiry into the Chinese culture and self does not lack differing views and empirical findings. By analyzing the Confucian *Analects,* the central text that records Confucius' teaching, scholars found well-preserved space for the individual, particularly with regard to the person's moral self-cultivation (Chang, 1997; King, 1985; C. F. Yang, 1993). In examining children's lives during the early twentieth century, Saari (1990) observed that Chinese children developed an "inner self" in order to retain a private space of their own. These scholars conclude that claiming that Confucian cultures only emphasize and impose social roles and hierarchy on people may be simplistic and one-sided.

Some empirical research also echoes these counterclaims. For example, Bond and Cheung (1983) documented that Chinese made the most references on several of their key individual dimensions while using the fewest social descriptors (compared to both Japanese and Americans). Furthermore, Lau (1992) also found that Chinese endorsed no fewer "individualistic" values than Americans, with Chinese scoring higher on some autonomous values such as "freedom" but lower on some typically collectivist values such as "family security." Even Harry Triandis's own research (Triandis, McCusker, and Hui, 1990) failed to support some of the key assumptions about the collectivist self; for example, Chinese displayed more self-reliance but less "social connection" (for instance, sense of belonging) than Americans.

Recent research also found that, despite their overall collectivist tendency, Chinese selves emphasize self-reliance, individual responsibility (Ho and Chiu, 1994), success, ambition, personal capability (Schwartz, 1994), personal agency, and even autonomy in decision making (Helwig, Arnold, Tan, and Boyd, 2003; Wink, Gao, Jones, and Chao, 1997). Most striking is the research by Y.-Y. Yang (2001), who documents that Chinese selves look more like web builders rather than fixed web nodes in their intricate social relations. They keep flexible interpersonal boundaries where they can bring strangers into their relation network and also be creative in pushing their so-called in-group members out if they don't want them. By doing so, Chinese selves display a great deal more personal agency than has been acknowledged.

Perhaps the most direct challenge comes from the research on Chinese children's consistently high school achievement (Harmon and others, 1997; Stevenson and Stigler, 1992). Yu (1996) has argued that Chinese achievement motivation is socially oriented. However, research by Stevenson and associates and others (for example, Hau and Salili, 1991) has repeatedly documented that Chinese children believe strongly in personal effort, a concept that clearly denotes individual agency. Li's recent examination of Chinese conceptions of learning (2002) also reveals a great deal of personal agency. Interestingly, researchers advocating for the collectivist Chinese self rarely acknowledge this very phenomenon and the potential discrepancy it poses for their claims.

These differing views and conflicting empirical findings cast doubt on the sharply and statically assumed distinctions between I-C selves. More and more scholars are calling this dichotomy into question. Some researchers have proposed that both types of self may coexist in any culture (Kagitçibasi, 1994; Ho and Chiu, 1994; Singelis, 1994). Others have gone further to argue that selves may be much more complex in meaning, dynamic in process, and variable from context to context (Helwig, Arnold, Tan, and Boyd, 2003; Turiel and Wainryb, 2000).

Aim of Our Research

We conducted two studies on Chinese adolescents' self-concepts in terms of individual and social orientation on the basis of two perspectives. First, we adopt the theoretical stance that selves in cultures are much more complex than the two dichotomous types can accommodate. We suspected that there are culturally specific conceptions of self among Chinese children that may have been overlooked in previous research. Second, we share the view that part of the complexity in self may be due to specific contexts and domains of activity in which individuals function rather than delineating self as a decontextualized entity (Helwig, Arnold, Tan, and Boyd, 2003; Yau and Smetana, 1996). This view assumes that selves, particularly with regard to their specific meanings, are not static notions but dynamically constructed and that they vary from domain to domain. In our study, we chose learning as a particular domain in an attempt to locate Chinese selves in a specific context.

Chinese Selves in the Domain of Learning

We chose the domain of learning because past research has consistently documented the essential role learning assumes in Chinese lives (Chao, 1996; Li, 2002, 2003b; Watkins and Biggs, 1996). The importance of learning is influenced by Confucian teaching of the concept *ren,* a lifelong striving for becoming the most genuine, sincere, and humane person one can become (Tu, 1979). This process is also called self-perfection and is believed possible for anyone who seeks it. This outline of life purposes and processes is deeply inspiring to the Chinese not only because it is for everyone but also because it is under each individual's control. Consequently, to the Chinese learning is not a mere academic pursuit but an individual moral striving as well. Li's study (2002) found that knowledge was more defined by college students as "a need to perfect oneself," a notion clearly reminiscent of Confucian moral self-striving, than "understanding the world," a more typical construal of knowledge in the West (Li, 2003b). Unfortunately, research adopting the I-C dichotomy has neglected to address this important dimension of Confucian influence on Chinese people and their self-concepts.

Modern formal learning complements the Confucian conception of self-perfection and is seen as an important part of this purpose because academic disciplines are the areas in which one needs to self-improve constantly (Li, 2002, 2003a; Ran, 2001; Watkins and Biggs, 1996). In this process, Chinese have been found to seek to develop what we term "learning virtues" of diligence, resolve, endurance of hardship, perseverance, and concentration (Hau and Salili, 1991; Li, 2001, 2002; Li and Wang, forthcoming; Stevenson and Stigler, 1992). These "learning virtues" constitute the core of Chinese personal agency in learning.

Recent research further shows that Chinese also emphasize personal competence, mastery, and achievement through learning (Li, 2002; Li and Fisher, 2004; Wink, Gao, Jones, and Chao, 1997). Moreover, learning is seen as a process that enables one to establish oneself socioeconomically (Li, 2002; Salili, Chiu, and Lai, 2001), that is, achieving self-sufficiency (Ho and Chiu, 1994). Finally, learning can bring satisfaction to one's own life, helping one to obtain a sense of fulfillment and happiness (Li and Wang, in press).

Whereas self-concepts encompass many dimensions, we sought to focus on two specific but core areas: goals of learning and sense of agency because they are most central to the self in the domain of learning. We focused on adolescents because it is a developmental period where one's sense of self is heightened. Moreover, adolescents are more adept in articulating their goals and agency in learning, thereby offering a unique window for exploring important self-concepts among Chinese children. We predicted that Chinese adolescents would hold a set of goals and express various aspects of their sense of agency that are both social and individual, reflecting their cultural values as well as their own thoughts of possible selves (Markus and Nurius, 1986). However, on the basis of the foregoing literature review, we anticipated more individual than social goals and agency in this domain, countering the collectivist claims. In addition, we also anticipated some within-culture differences between grades and boys and girls.

Method and Data: Study One

To tap Chinese adolescents' goals of learning and sense of agency, we first used an open-ended method, followed by close-ended methods based on the findings culled from our first study.

In the first study, we collected data from a total of 187 twelve-to-fifteen-year-olds attending seventh, eighth, and ninth grade, with 84 in seventh, 80 in eighth, and 23 in ninth grade; there were 78 boys and 109 girls from five regions of China. All participants were from city schools and middle-income families, reflecting the majority of Chinese city population (NCEDR, 2001).

We developed a questionnaire that probed, in writing, participants' goals of learning and sense of agency in learning. Four questions were used to elicit goals of learning:

1. What does knowledge mean to you?
2. Do you need to learn? Rate yourself on a 5-point scale from "not at all" to "very much." (If participants rated higher than 2, they were asked to respond to the next question, "Why do you need to learn?" which was used as our second open-ended question.)
3. How would you be if one day you could not learn anymore?
4. Do you like learning? Rate yourself on a 5-point scale from "not at all" to "very much."

Regardless of their responses, participants were asked to respond to "Why did you give yourself this rating?" with only that as our final question.

For agency in learning, we used five open-ended questions:

1. How do you learn when you are faced with difficulties in learning (e.g., you don't understand the teacher or your homework)?
2. How do you learn when you fail?
3. How do you learn when, after you've tried hard, you still can't seem to learn?
4. How do you learn when you achieve well (e.g., high score on a test or teacher praise)?
5. Sometimes, you may not have an interest in some things. How do you learn then?

We took two steps to code our data: establishing coding schemes, and actual coding. For the former, we adopted techniques of content analysis (Shaver, Schwartz, Kirson, and O'Connor, 1987) and systematically identified goals of learning and expressions of personal agency. Accordingly, three coders, blind to our hypotheses, read independently a random sample of 20 percent of the raw data. First, they each recorded "distinct" goals and types of agency. The distinctness of a goal or type of agency was defined as being not interchangeable with another (Shaver, Schwartz, Kirson, and O'Connor, 1987). For example, "my goal of learning is to know a lot about the world" and "my goal is to help my parents" were seen by the coders as two distinct goals. Likewise, "I persist in the face of difficulty" and "I work on a school problem independently first" were also seen as two types of agency with the first focusing on persistence and the second on independence.

When at least two of the three coders noted the same goal or type of agency from the same adolescent, that item was entered on the item list. For items lacking agreement, the coders discussed and excluded them if disagreement remained. Next, the coders independently examined the entries on the list and grouped them into conceptually similar categories. At the end, the three coders grouped individual versus social categories, for goals and agency respectively.

This cyclical, multileveled procedure led to establishment of nine categories of goals, six of which were deemed individual and three social. Whereas some of these categories had subcategories, others did not. Similarly, this procedure produced six categories of agency, four of which were deemed individual and two social. Most categories of agency also contained subcategories. Any adolescent could have expressed any number of these goals and any type of agency. Table 2.1 shows these goals and types of agency, which we describe next.

Goals of Learning. With respect to individual goals of learning, the first category, "cognitive goals," had three component goals. The first, "to develop one's ability/competence/skills," emphasized developing the self's own ability (for example, "I want to have skills to solve many problems in life"). The second subgoal involved "expanding one's horizons and worldview." This goal stressed the need to increase the self's knowledge in ever-expanding quantity and ever-varying spheres of life (for example, "I want to expand my view beyond where I came from all the way into the world"). The third subgoal was to "master knowledge" so that the self could possess it to serve the self's needs in life (for example, "I need to master knowledge so that it's in my own head at my beck and call").

The second category of goals, also with three subgoals, was organized around the notion of "aspirations." The first subgoal, "to keep the self's ideal, aspiration, and ambition," referred to long-range goals (for example, "My goal of learning is to be famous"). The second subgoal consisted of the desire to "have accomplishments in life for the self" (for example, "I want to achieve excellence in life"). The third subgoal involved the desire to "self-strengthen continuously without ever stopping"; this goal reflects the pursuit of learning as a lifelong process (as in "I will learn as long as I live").

The third category was organized around the goal of achieving "moral/spiritual/wisdom," also with three subgoals. The first involved the intention to "forge the self's moral character," which consists of improving the self in the moral domain (for example, "I learn so that I can distinguish right from wrong"). The second subgoal, "enriching the self's life," was aimed at

Table 2.1. Self's Individual and Social Goals and Agency in Learning Expressed by Chinese Adolescents

	Goals of Learning	Agency in Learning
Individual	Cognitive goals 　Develop self's ability/competence/skills 　Expand self's horizons/worldview 　Master knowledge for self Aspirations 　Keep self's ideal/aspiration/ambition 　Have accomplishments in life for self 　Self-strengthen without ever stopping Moral/spiritual/wisdom 　Forge self's moral character 　Enrich self's life 　Obtain wisdom for self 　Experience love/happiness/enjoyment for self 　Elevate self's SES 　Learning is good for self in general	General effort 　Be diligent 　Have resolve 　Endure hardship 　Persevere 　Concentrate 　Remain humble Self-generate/regulate learning 　Set goals for self 　Use strategies to achieve goals 　Regulate self's emotions 　Compete with others (to be better oneself)
Social	Benefit others 　Contribute to society 　Honor parents and teachers 　Not become a burden to society Streamline self with social world 　Keep up with societal development 　Catch up with others 　Receive social acceptance 　Develop interpersonal relationships	Seek help from others Interact with others Study/discuss with/emulate others Participate in social activities

finding meaning in life or seeking spirituality (for example, "If I don't learn, I feel empty, and I feel my life is being wasted"). The third subgoal, "obtaining wisdom," involved seeking deeper understanding of the human world.

The fourth category consisted of "experiencing love/happiness/enjoyment" with learning (for example, "I am very happy when I learn"). The fifth category was organized around attempts to "elevate one's SES" (for example, "I want to make a lot of money"). Finally, the sixth category involved a general notion that learning is "good for oneself" in all aspects.

With regard to social goals, the first category involved "benefiting others." Participants indicated three subgoal types. The first involved the desire to "contribute to society," including the self's own community, country, and the world at large (for example, "I want to help educate our country's poor children"). The second subgoal was to "honor the self's parents and teachers," who nurtured the self in his or her development, such as "my parents sacrificed for my education; I want to bring honor to and take care of them." The third subgoal was organized around not becoming a "burden to society." (This goal was coded as a type of social goal because the self adopted a societal perspective.)

The second category of social goals involved "streamlining the self with the social world." Again, this category was embodied by three subgoals. The first was to "keep up with societal development" so that the self would be part of the development (for example, "computer science is developing fast now, but I need to learn that so that I won't be left behind"). The second reflected a desire to "catch up with others" in order to compete and surpass others in learning. (This goal is defined in terms of how the self is compared with others). The third subgoal was embodied by a need to "receive social acceptance" such as respect, honor, and recognition. Finally, the third category consisted of "developing interpersonal relationships" (for example "I will know how to make more friends").

Agency in Learning. As shown in Table 2.1, the first of the four individual categories of agency was the general notion of effort, which referred to individual striving and working hard toward the self's goal. There were five components specifying particular dimensions of effort. "Be diligent" (*qin*) was the first, which stressed the need for frequent studying (for example, "I always study no matter what happens"). The second consisted of "having resolve" (*fen*). *Fen* refers to one's commitment to a course of learning and reflects a certain "stubbornness" in serious, intense, but optimistic pursuit of the self's goals (for example, "I have the resolve to realize my dream of becoming a lawyer"). The third component consists of "enduring hardship" (*keku*); it addressed the self's staunch attitude and behavioral tendency toward overcoming difficulties that were the opposite of fun, pleasure, or luxury. These difficulties ranged from poverty and difficult knowledge to the self's perceived lack of intelligence (for example, "My family is poor, but I save money from food to buy books. I must endure this hardship"). The fourth component involves the desire to "persevere" (*hengxin*). *Hengxin* corresponds to what the self does to continue learning when faced with failures, as in "I failed the exam. But I will never give up; I will continue to study hard again." The final component was "concentration" (*zhuanxin*), where the self tried to pay undivided attention to his or her learning. For example, "Whenever I study, I put my whole heart and mind to the work."

The second large category of agency was organized around the ideal "remaining humble." Humility consists of the need and readiness to learn from any source or from any person, which functions to prevent the self from becoming arrogant or conceited (for example, "It's important to remain humble so I won't be full of myself"). We classified humility as an agentic subcategory in light of its capacity to sustain adolescents' attempts toward self-improvement.

The third category of agency consists of "self-generated/self-regulated learning." This category pertains to specific types of activities the *self* generates or controls, and not to those that were merely intended to meet contextual demands (such as going to school or doing homework). There were also three activity types in this category. First involves "setting learning goals for the self" (for example, "I set my own goal for memorizing five English words a day"). The second type consisted of "using strategies to achieve the self's goals," such as reviewing course material before and after class and using flashcards. The third type included "regulating the self's emotions," in which participants referred to strategies for handling the self's emotional reactions to failure or setbacks. Examples of such regulation included actively encouraging the self to increase confidence, and trying to think positively.

The fourth and final category of agency involved the need to "compete with others" in order to achieve the self's best. For example, one participant indicated that "competition makes me want to do my best. Even if I don't make it to the top, I feel I would win in the end."

With regard to social agency, there were two categories. The first was "seeking help from others," which indicated that one's learning benefits from seeking and receiving support from others. For example, "I ask for help if I can't figure out something by myself." The second category consisted of social interaction, of which there were two components. The first involved the proclivity to "study and discuss with others as well as emulate others' examples" (for example, "I like to discuss and debate with my peers"). The second was "participating in social activities." Usually adolescents referred to activities in which they were engaged outside of school (such as community service or activities at the workplace where the self's book knowledge can be used and verified).

We used these categories and components to code the data. First we achieved reliability by having two coders, who had no knowledge of our predictions, code a random sample of the data. Real coding began upon reaching high reliability scores for goals and agency (Cohen's kappa = .83 and .89 respectively).

Findings and Discussion. From Table 2.1, it is clear that regarding goals and agency there were individual and social references. This lent support for the argument that both types of orientations coexist. However, in goals and agency alike, there were more, not fewer, types of individual categories than social categories (for goals, mean = 5.92 compared to 1.40; for agency, mean = 6.98 compared to 1.56, respectively). To test for group differences between boys and girls and across the three grades in the outcome variables (the categories), we performed analyses of variance (ANOVAs). We found again that as a whole (all individual and social goals aggregated respectively) these adolescents expressed more individual goals than social goals and sense of agency. Gender and grades did not differ.

Within the categories of goals and agency, we also tested for group differences by gender and grade and found some. On the one hand, seventh graders referred to more individual cognitive goals, but eighth graders harbored more goals for elevating their SES, and ninth graders expressed more individual aspirations. On the other hand, girls articulated more individual moral/spiritual goals than boys. However, ninth grade boys mentioned more love, happiness, and enjoyment for learning than girls, whereas the other two grades did not differ. Interestingly, none of the social goals showed any differences. Concerning agency, girls in the ninth grade showed a higher level of personal effort than boys, but there were no gender differences in the other grades. No differences were found for humility, self-generated/regulated learning, or seeking help.

It appeared that there was more variability within the individual orientation for both goals and agency than within the social orientation. These findings supported our general argument that selves in any culture are more complex than has been acknowledged by researchers of the I-C persuasion.

Methods and Data: Study Two

The purpose of study two was to further verify what we found in our first study. Even though we detected clear patterns of Chinese adolescents' strong individual orientation in study one, the open-ended method may not have provided participants equal opportunity to consider both individual and social aspects of their own learning. We sought to collect more direct and focused data on their references to self in this domain. Therefore, on the basis of the content of participants' responses in study one, we developed twenty-two statements about the self's attitudes toward and behavioral tendencies in learning. Half of the twenty-two statements showed individual orientation and half showed social orientation within an identical aspect of learning. Examples are "My learning is my own business; it has nothing to do with others" (tapping individual orientation) versus "My learning has a lot to do with others; it's not just my own business" (tapping social orientation), or "I like to study alone" (individual) versus "I like to study with other people" (social). These statements were randomly ordered. The statements as a whole cohered (internal consistency) moderately well (XX = .65 for the individual items and .60 for the social items).

A second group of adolescents (52 seventh graders and 114 eighth graders, 78 boys and 88 girls, for a total of 166) from similar demographic backgrounds were asked to rate themselves on a 5-point scale. Their ratings ranged from "completely agree" to "do not agree at all" for statements that focused on adolescents' attitudes toward learning, and "always describes me" to "never describes me" for statements that focused on their behavioral tendencies. To reduce social desirability, participants responded to our scales anonymously.

In terms of findings, the mean rating for individual orientation was 3.43 and for social orientation 2.24. Our analyses showed again that adolescents rated individual orientation significantly higher than social orientation. There were no differences between the boys and girls or the two grades, or any interactions between these factors. These findings generally confirmed the results of our study one.

General Discussion

Our goal in this research was to examine two particularly important areas of Chinese adolescents' self-concepts: goals and agency in the domain of learning. We took the theoretical perspective that selves in any culture are more complex than the I-C framework has acknowledged. One way selves in cultures are complex may have to do with the *content*, not just the structure and process, of self-concepts that are informed by specific cultural values. Whereas structure and process (Bracken, 1996; Harter, 1998) are important in describing selves, content is equally important. Content is about meanings that individuals construct about themselves. According to cultural psychologists, meanings are indispensable in examining selves because they exert what D'Andrade (1987) called "directive force" or motivation for behavior.

Our data supported not only our prediction that there would be more individual goals and agency but also the idea that there were culturally specific meanings Chinese adolescents would express in their goals and related agency. We did not find a few individual goals, but rather six categories consisting of twelve distinguishable goals these adolescents harbored about their purposes of learning. Adding the three categories of seven specific social goals, there were nineteen goals. Even though no single adolescent expressed all nineteen, the majority of them (78 percent) expressed four or more, and 41 percent had six or more. Only 7 percent had fewer than two goals. The same picture applied to agency. Our data showed four categories of individual agency, consisting of eleven specific types. Adding the three social types of agency, there were fourteen in total. Again, no single adolescent mentioned all of these types, but 85 percent of them mentioned four or more, and 50 percent mentioned six or more. Only 4 percent mentioned fewer than two types of agency.

From a cultural perspective, we argue that these categories of goals and agency reflect well the Chinese cultural value system regarding learning, which is largely Confucian (Li, 2002; Tu, 1979; Watkins and Biggs, 1996). Accordingly, the fundamental purpose of learning is geared toward the notion of self-perfection, which stresses the role of the individual, particularly his or her decision, commitment, and day-to-day practice throughout life. Learning is believed to be the only underlying process that can lead the individual toward that ultimate goal.

Because of the centrality learning assumes in this process, individual goals and agency are only natural results. Furthermore, learning was also historically linked to "civil service" through China's examination system (from the seventh century to the turn of the twentieth), which was inevitably associated with status, honor, and practical benefits. Modern learning through schooling as imported from the West achieved added significance in the hearts and minds of Chinese people. The multifaceted nature of goals and types of agency found in this research reflect these complex cultural, historical, and social influences. Therefore, they must be studied in their own right. Reducing these rich goals and types of agency to the I-C dichotomy is doing gross injustice to self-concepts of Chinese people.

A second way selves in cultures are complex may be due to the particular domains of human activity and psychological functioning. Even though people do have abstract notions of themselves, they are at any given moment of the day likely to carry out activities in specific contexts or domains. Since human activities are not random but socially organized, most often these contexts and domains recur regularly, such as going to work and coming home as a daily routine. Likewise, children spend most of their waking time learning in school. Because contexts and domains have their own purposes, processes, and demands, individuals' self-concepts are bound to differ from one context to another (Helwig, Arnold, Tan, and Boyd, 2003; Yau and Smetana, 1996). These domain-specific, rather than global abstract, self-concepts may be more potent in influencing behavior and performance outcomes (Bracken, 1996; Harter, 1998). Domain-specific differences among individuals may constitute one dimension or level where the dynamism in the construction of self-concepts is generated.

Learning (informal and formal) is a domain for any culture but is distinct for the Chinese for reasons we have stated. At the general level across cultures, learning—especially formal learning—as a unique domain calls upon more individual participation and processes. No matter how the social context for learning is structured, the individual is the agent that must be actively engaged in the activity for learning to take place. Therefore, learning is a prime domain for investigating children's self-concepts in a so-called collectivist culture. It is therefore reasonable to assume that this domain mostly pulls out children's self-concepts about their mental capacity and achievement. Whereas this is generally the case in the West (Bracken, 1996; Harter, 1998), research since the 1980s, surprisingly, shows that this is not the case with Asians (Stevenson and Stigler, 1992; Hau and Salili, 1991; Li, 2002, 2003b). Asian adults and children emphasize personal effort more than their mental ability in learning. Thus, even though learning may possess some common features that distinguish it from other domains (such as family life), this domain may still show configurations and meanings that vary with cultural values and practices.

Our data supported the domain-specific argument at both the general and cultural levels. At the general level (that is, regardless of cultural differences), our findings showed more individual than social orientation in both goals and agency. This was rather startling considering the verdict that the I-C framework has cast on Chinese people's collectivist selves. Why did both studies produce the same reversed orientations? If previous research results based on the I-C framework have validity, it may be that they either tapped the global, abstract self-concepts of the Chinese (Bond and Forgas, 1984; Triandis, McCusker, and Hui, 1990) or they tapped the social and interpersonal domains (Leung and Bond, 1984; Wheeler, Reis, and Bond,

1989). By changing the focus to a particular domain, we found very different patterns. This may well be attributable to the fact that learning is a common domain where individual goals and agency are necessary if anyone is to function. Inevitably, the domain-specific approach poses challenges to the I-C framework.

At the cultural level, these reversed findings with their specific configurations and meanings attest to the argument that learning as a domain may still differ from culture to culture despite its commonality across cultures. For example, a significant component of Chinese adolescents' goals for learning was to cultivate oneself morally and spiritually. Many of the actual words adolescents used reflected Confucian such expressions as perfecting oneself (*ziwo wanshan*) and elevating the self's moral character (*tigao zijide pinde*). This also applied to agency. For example, the five types of agency (diligence, resolve, endurance of hardship, perseverance, and concentration) and humility constituted a large proportion of Chinese adolescents' sense of agency in learning. These particular forms of agency also mirrored Confucian terms of the so-called learning virtues that have been documented repeatedly (Li, 2001, 2002, 2003a, 2003b). It is not the general notion of "effort" per se but these culturally specific agentic processes the self initiates that are likely to produce behavior and outcomes. Thus, domains and contexts of human activities and psychological functioning may differ in specific ways that can influence people's self-concepts in that domain. It is particularly important to study culturally specific ways.

A third way selves in cultures may be complex is that there are bound to be differences within cultures. Even though there may be some large cross-cultural tendencies in self-orientation from the I-C perspective, we stand to gain much understanding from examining variations within cultures. So long as psychology's primary anchor is the individual, within-culture variations must not be neglected at the expense of large cultural tendencies. Our research yielded some initial data on differences among Chinese adolescents. First, we found more variability within individual than social orientation; that is, adolescents' goals and sense of agency differed by grade and gender for some individual goals and types of agency, but not for their social goals and agency. Our sample consisted of only middle-class city residents; therefore we could not analyze differences associated with SES, rural versus city residence, or developed versus underdeveloped regions (these are known factors that influence people's lives in China; NCEDR, 2001). However, we included enough boys and girls to explore possible gender differences. Indeed, we found some. For example, girls as a whole expressed more individual moral/spiritual goals than boys. Within the ninth grade, boys mentioned more love, happiness, and enjoyment, but girls in this grade articulated more personal effort than boys. These differences may mean that girls care more about the moral/spiritual purposes of learning relative to boys and boys find positive affect more important relative to girls.

Although these results were hard to interpret accurately, within-culture variations do exist and merit more research.

Finally, the complexity in self and culture may also be due to developmental processes. At various developmental points, children in different cultures may be socialized to master certain tasks deemed important by their own cultures. In the domain of learning, for example, Chao (1996) found that whereas Euro-American mothers regarded self-esteem, social skills, and having fun to be important goals for their preschool children's success in school, their Chinese American counterparts named hard work as the most important attitude for their children to develop. Chao's recent research (2000) also documented that Chinese American parents expected their adolescent children to be fully self-reliant in their schoolwork, which is a key reason these parents did not think they needed to be involved in their children's school. Therefore, developmental changes in adolescents' self-concepts in learning are expected.

We used grade as a proxy for age because we examined the domain of learning, which we assumed centrally reflected children's learning experiences from grade to grade rather than increased age per se. Whereas most of the categories did not differ by grade, we did find some grade-related variations, which may indicate developmental trends. For example, seventh graders referred to more individual cognitive goals, but their ninth grade peers expressed more individual aspirations. The higher frequency of cognitive goals among seventh graders was sensible considering that they were entering their first year of middle school, where the curriculum was much more demanding than in elementary school (Stevenson and Stigler, 1992). Developing one's ability and mastering knowledge might indeed be deemed as more important by seventh graders than by their peers in higher grades of middle school. By ninth grade, adolescents faced another examination designed to select higher achievers into college-bound high school, where fierce competition was (and still is) an unavoidable social reality. Adolescents might in fact receive more concerted messages from their parents, school, and culture at large about their future. It seems also sensible for them to ponder and project future-oriented aspirations. However, we are fully aware that we found few developmental differences, which did not enable us to interpret these findings accurately. Still, developmentally related changes are likely to exist in this domain, and future research needs to investigate this area.

Selves in cultures and their development are important research topics. The research produced in the I-C paradigm ushered in the inquiry into the role culture plays in the construction of self. More recent research, however, shows that selves are more complex than the I-C dichotomy has acknowledged. The present research adopted another approach, that of a particular domain, to investigate Chinese adolescents' goals of learning and sense of agency. We collected these adolescents' self-descriptions as anchored in the specific domain of learning. We found differing patterns of their self-concepts, which were also confirmed by a set of data. These findings broadened our understanding of selves in Chinese culture. Admittedly, no single approach will reveal the full intricacies and dynamic processes of selves. Nonetheless, we can move closer to them if we continue to inquire into the whole spectrum of selves and their developments from multiple perspectives.

References

Bond, M. H., and Cheung, T. "College Students' Spontaneous Self-Concept: The Effects of Culture Among Respondents in Hong Kong, Japan, and the United States." *Journal of Cross-Cultural Psychology*, 1983, *14*, 153–171.

Bond, M. H., and Forgas, J. P. "Linking Personal Perception to Behavior Intention Across Cultures: The Role of Cultural Collectivism." *Journal of Cross-Cultural Psychology*, 1984, *15*, 337–352.

Bracken, B. "Clinical Applications of a Context-Dependent Multi-Dimensional Model of Self-Concept." In B. Bracken (ed.), *Handbook of Self-Concept*. New York: Wiley, 1996.

Chang, H. C. "Language and Words: Communication in the *Analects* of Confucius." *Journal of Language and Social Psychology*, 1997, *16*, 107–131.

Chao, R. K. "Chinese and European American Mothers' Views About the Role of Parenting in Children's School Success." *Journal of Cross-Cultural Psychology*, 1996, *27*, 403–423.

Chao, R. K. "Cultural Explanation for the Role of Parenting in the School Success of Asian American Children." In R. Taylor and M. Wang (eds.), *Resilience Across Contexts: Family, Work, Culture, and Community*. Mahwah, N.J.: Erlbaum, 2000.

D'Andrade, R. "A Folk Model of the Mind." In D. Holland and N. Quinn (eds.), *Cultural Models in Language and Thought*. Cambridge: Cambridge University Press, 1987.

Harmon, M., and others. *Performance Assessment in IEA's Third International Mathematics and Science Study (TIMSS)*. Chestnut Hill, Mass.: TIMSS International Study Center, Boston College, 1997.

Harter, S. "The Development of Self-Representations." In W. Damon (series ed.) and N. Eisenberg (vol. ed.), *Handbook of Child Psychology, Vol. 3*. (5th ed.) New York: Wiley, 1998.

Hau, K. T., and Salili, F. "Structure and Semantic Differential Placement of Specific Causes: Academic Causal Attributions by Chinese Students in Hong Kong." *International Journal of Psychology*, 1991, *26*, 175–193.

Helwig, C. C., Arnold, M. L., Tan, D-.L., and Boyd, D. "Chinese Adolescents' Reasoning About Democratic and Authority-Based Decision Making in Peer, Family, and School Contexts." *Child Development*, 2003, *74*(3), 783–800.

Ho, D.Y.F. "Chinese Patterns of Socialization: A Critical Review." In M. Bond (ed.), *The Psychology of the Chinese People*. Hong Kong: Oxford University Press, 1986.

Ho, D.Y.F., and Chiu, C. Y. "Component Ideas of Individualism, Collectivism, and Social Organization: An Application in the Study of Chinese Culture." In U. Kim and others (eds.), *Individualism and Collectivism: Theory, Method, and Applications*. Thousand Oaks, Calif.: Sage, 1994.

Hofstede, G. *Culture's Consequences: International Differences in Work-Related Values*. Thousand Oaks, Calif.: Sage, 1980.

Hsu, F.L.K. *Americans and Chinese: Passage to Difference*. (3rd ed.) Honolulu: University of Hawaii, 1981.

Hui, C. H., and Triandis, H. "Individualism and Collectivism: A Study of Cross-Cultural Researchers." *Journal of Cross-Cultural Psychology*, 1986, *17*, 225–248.

Kagitçibasi, Ç. "A Critical Appraisal of Individualism and Collectivism: Toward a New Formulation." In U. Kim and others (eds.), *Individualism and Collectivism: Theory, Method, and Applications.* Thousand Oaks, Calif.: Sage, 1994.

King, A.Y.C. "The Individual and Group in Confucianism: A Relational Perspective." In D. H. Munroe (ed.), *Individualism and Holism: Studies in Confucian and Taoist Values.* Ann Arbor: University of Michigan Press, 1985.

Lau, S. "Collectivism's Individualism: Value Preference, Personal Control, and the Desire for Freedom Among Chinese in Mainland China, Hong Kong, and Singapore." *Personality and Individual Differences,* 1992, *13,* 361–366.

Leung, K., and Bond, M. H. "The Impact of Cultural Collectivism on Reward Allocation." *Journal of Personality and Social Psychology,* 1984, *4,* 793–804.

Li, J. "Chinese Conceptualization of Learning." *Ethos,* 2001, *29,* 111–137.

Li, J. "A Cultural Model of Learning: Chinese 'Heart and Mind for Wanting to Learn.'" *Journal of Cross-Cultural Psychology,* 2002, *33*(3), 248–269.

Li, J. "The Core of Confucian Learning." *American Psychologist,* 2003a, *58,* 146–147.

Li, J. "U.S. and Chinese Cultural Beliefs About Learning." *Journal of Educational Psychology,* 2003b, *95*(2), 258–267.

Li, J., and Fischer, K. W. "Thoughts and Emotions in American and Chinese Cultural Beliefs About Learning." In D. Y. Dai and R. Sternberg (eds.), *Motivation, Emotion, and Cognition: Integrative Perspectives on Intellectual Functioning.* Mahwah, N.J.: Erlbaum, 2004.

Li, J., and Wang, Q. "U.S. and Chinese Preschool Children's Perceptions of Achievement and Their Achieving Peers." *Social Development,* forthcoming.

Markus, H. J., and Kitayama, S. "Culture and the Self: Implications for Cognition, Emotion and Motivation." *Psychological Review,* 1991, *98*(2), 224–253.

Markus, H. R., and Nurius, P. "Possible Selves." *American Psychologist,* 1986, *41,* 954–969.

Menon, T., Morris, M. W., Chiu, C.-Y., and Hong, Y.-Y. "Culture and Construal of Agency: Attribution to Individual Versus Group Dispositions." *Journal of Personality and Social Psychology,* 1999, *76,* 701–717.

NCEDR (National Center for Education Development Research). *2001 Green Paper on Education in China: Annual Report on Policies of China's Education* [in Chinese]. Beijing, China: Educational Science Publishing House, 2001.

Ran, A. "Travelling on Parallel Tracks: Chinese Parents and English Teachers." *Educational Research,* 2001, *43,* 311–328.

Saari, J. L. *Legacies of Childhood: Growing up Chinese in a Time of Crisis 1890–1920.* Cambridge, Mass.: Council on East-Asian Studies, Harvard University, 1990.

Salili, F., Chiu, C. Y., and Lai, S. "The Influence of Culture and Context on Students' Achievement Orientations." In F. Salili, C. Y. Chiu, and Y. Y. Hong (eds.), *Student Motivation: The Culture and Context of Learning.* New York: Plenum, 2001.

Schwartz, S. H. "Beyond Individualism/Collectivism: New Cultural Dimensions of Values." In U. Kim and others (eds.), *Individualism and Collectivism: Theory, Method, and Applications.* Thousand Oaks, Calif.: Sage, 1994.

Shaver, P., Schwartz, J., Kirson, D., and O'Connor, C. "Emotion Knowledge: Further Exploration of a Prototype Approach." *Journal of Personality and Social Psychology,* 1987, *52,* 1061–1086.

Singelis, T. M. "The Measurement of Independent and Interdependent Self-Construals." *Personality and Social Psychology Bulletin,* 1994, *20,* 580–607.

Stevenson, H. W., and Stigler, J. W. *The Learning Gap.* New York: Simon & Schuster, 1992.

Triandis, H. C. *Individualism and Collectivism.* Boulder, Colo.: Westview, 1995.

Triandis, H., McCusker, C., and Hui, C. "Multimethod Probes of Individualism and Collectivism." *Journal of Personality and Social Psychology,* 1990, *54,* 323–338.

Tu, W. M. *Humanity and Self-Cultivation: Essays in Confucian Thought.* Berkeley, Calif.: Asian Humanities Press, 1979.

Turiel, E., and Wainryb, C. "Social Life in Cultures: Judgments, Conflict, and Subversion." *Child Development*, 2000, *71*, 250–256.

Wang, Q. "Cultural Effects on Adults' Earliest Childhood Recollection and Self-Description: Implications for the Relation Between Memory and the Self." *Journal of Personality and Social Psychology*, 2001, *81*, 220–233.

Watkins, D. A., and Biggs, J. B. (eds.). *The Chinese Learner: Cultural, Psychological, and Contextual Influences*. Hong Kong: Comparative Education Research Centre, 1996.

Wheeler, L., Reis, H. T., and Bond, M. H. "Collectivism-Individualism in Everyday Social Life: The Middle Kingdom and the Melting Pot." *Journal of Personality and Social Psychology*, 1989, *57*, 79–86.

Wink, P., Gao, B., Jones, S., and Chao, F. "Social Values and Relationships with Parents Among American College Women of Chinese and European Descent." *International Journal of Psychology*, 1997, *32*, 169–179.

Yang, C. F. "Are Chinese People Really 'Collectivist?' On Chinese Cultural Value System." In K. S. Yang (ed.), *Chinese Values from the Perspective of Social Science* [in Chinese]. Taipei, Taiwan: Guiguan, 1993.

Yang, K. S. "Theories and Research in Chinese Personality: An Indigenous Approach." In H.S.R. Kao and D. Sinha (eds.), *Asian Perspectives on Psychology: Cross-Cultural Research and Methodology Series, Vol. 19*. New Delhi, India: Sage, 1997.

Yang, Y.-Y. "One of Us (Zijiren): A Case Study on the Classification of Chinese Guanxi" [in Chinese]. *Indigenous Psychological Research in Chinese Societies*, 2001, *13*, 277–316.

Yau, J., and Smetana, J. G. "Adolescent-Parent Conflict Among Chinese Adolescents in Hong Kong." *Child Development*, 1996, *67*, 1262–1275.

Yu, A. B. "Ultimate Life Concerns, Self, and Chinese Achievement Motivation." In M. Bond (ed.), *The Handbook of Chinese Psychology*. Hong Kong: Oxford University Press, 1996.

JIN LI is associate professor of education and human development at Brown University in Providence, Rhode Island.

XIAODONG YUE is assistant professor of psychology at the City University of Hong Kong.

This chapter introduces ways to conceptualize and measure the multiplicity of ethnic identifications among elementary-school-aged children of color and children from immigrant families.

Multiplicity of Ethnic Identification During Middle Childhood: Conceptual and Methodological Considerations

Daisuke Akiba, Laura A. Szalacha,
Cynthia T. García Coll

One of the milestones of child development involves a developing sense of self (Eder, 1989). Children in early middle childhood begin to synthesize various dimensions of the self, extending beyond concrete descriptions such as their names and physical characteristics to include such dimensions as attitudinal, behavioral, and cognitive characteristics and affiliation to social groups (Damon and Hart, 1988; Harter, 1996; Szkrybalo and Ruble, 1999). Thus, middle childhood represents the emergence of an adultlike construction of self. Many scholars agree that the self contains two aspects, a personal self and a social self; the latter is relevant in discussing ethnic identity, which involves classifying oneself on the basis of social groups (Cross, 1991; Ruble and others, 2004). Consequently, middle childhood may be an ideal age range during which to examine the development of ethnic identity; however, as illustrated in this chapter, research on the topic has not systematically focused on this age group.

Earlier Research on Ethnic Identity Development

Psychological investigations on ethnic identity development date back to the 1930s (for example, Clark and Clark, 1939; Horowitz, 1939); yet there are some methodological and conceptual concerns that call for further investigation. In her seminal work on ethnic identity among African American preschool children, Horowitz (1939) drew a culturally naïve conclusion that

African American children—and adults—rejected their own race; it was based on observation of their preferences among white and black figure drawings. Continuing this tradition, Clark and Clark (1947) presented African American children with a white doll and a black doll and concluded that young African American children often identified with black dolls while indicating preferences for white dolls. Branch and Newcombe (1986) discussed a variety of potential problems with this method: (1) children's familiarity with white-looking dolls being confounded with children's preference, (2) the preference for white dolls not being indicative of the preference for the white race, and (3) the dolls' skin colors not equivalent to the notion of race. Obviously, this approach or its derivatives may not effectively be applied to other groups, whose collective experiences may be even less meaningful in terms of a set of visual dimensions.

We expand on these concerns and propose that the dichotomization of race into a forced choice raises other methodological and conceptual issues. For one, it is our view that this accuracy-oriented dilemma model fails to accommodate the complexity of ethnic identity within each child, particularly in today's more-diverse-than-ever societies. There has been a prevalent tendency in psychology whereby researchers are unwarranted in attributing any psychosocial characteristics of persons of color to their racial or ethnic background, without considering a variety of factors, such as other social groups and identity dimensions, along which they may define themselves (Akiba and García Coll, 2003; Gibbs and Huang, 1989; McLoyd, 1999). This "color obsession" may have led to the assumption that, for example, the identity development of Latino youths is meaningfully conceptualized along a singular dimension—their identity as "Hispanic" (see Phinney, 1989). However, this socially constructed and imposed terminology may mean little to those in the Latino communities, who might instead identify in terms of their racial, national, and regional backgrounds (Waters, 1996). Thus, it should be noted that quantifying the "Hispanic identity" per se might not be useful in characterizing identity development among Latino children, especially the framework of a dilemma model. Hence a measure of ethnic identity is most useful if it accommodates a multitude of identity dimensions within each person.

At the same time, it should be noted that probing the constructs of a child's identity (that is, why does a Latino boy select "black" to describe himself?) would also be highly informative in assessing the reasoning behind the labels they select—regardless of their ostensible accuracy. Spencer (1985) points out that research on ethnic identity has rarely focused on construal of ethnic group identity. Investigating such dimensions would further facilitate our understanding of the development of ethnic identity.

In addition, it is important that researchers include a wider range of ages and other children of color. Branch (1999) points out that the results from earlier studies (for example, Horowitz, 1939) are frequently generalized to all people of color of all ages, despite the fact they only included African American children in early middle childhood. Spencer (1985) reminds us, however, that the processes of ethnic identity development begin at birth and continue throughout one's life. Also, generalization of the findings to others on the basis of African American children is unwarranted, as their experiences differ greatly and they cannot simply be treated as aggregate "minorities." In particular, with an increase in immigration from non-European nations, systematic consideration of children from immigrant backgrounds has become a necessary step in order to advance our conceptualization of ethnic identities. Suarez-Orozco and Suarez-Orozco (2002) inform us that, unlike immigrants entering the United States a few decades ago, immigrants today enter a society that permits them to retain their "original" cultural identities. This, however, must be interpreted in the context of a larger society that frequently devalues the cultural baggage with which these immigrants and their families may be associated.

It is therefore not surprising that the works by the Clarks (1947) and Horowitz (1939) are no longer considered adequate; however, it is important to realize that they are among the few empirical attempts at examining ethnic identity development, and that they offer some useful distinctions in conceptualizing the notion of ethnic identity (for example, identification versus preference). In the next section, we examine theories that explicitly address the developmental issues.

The Developmental Focus

Ethnic identity is often discussed within general theories of identity development, which typically focuses on teenagers exploring a variety of potential identities (Erikson, 1968; Marcia, 1980), but such discussions frequently lack conviction. For example, it automatically precludes preadolescents, since explorations usually only intensify in adolescence (Branch, 1999), which leaves us without a systematic understanding of how the notion of "ethnic self" emerges in children. Also, these theories' reliance on exploration may lead us to overestimate the power of volitional control. Even if a person of color chooses to actively deny her own racial background, she is likely to continue to experience life as a person of color. No matter how subtle such experiences may be, her identity cannot be understood solely in terms of choices grounded in individual effort. Other researchers have since extended on the Eriksonian theories and developed models that are specific to understanding identity development among people of color.

Helms (1994) and Cross (1971) theorized ethnic identity development among African Americans. Following the Eriksonian focus on exploration, these theories are founded upon the assumption that the critical steps of ethnic identity development take place primarily during adolescence; as such, much of their contribution is beyond the scope of the current manuscript. Cross, Parham, and Helms (1998) offer a comprehensive review of identity development among African Americans, mostly adolescents and adults (interested readers should consult their review). Cross (1971) and Helms (1994) both unambiguously warn us that this model is strictly designed to describe the psychology of African Americans; however, like the findings by Clark and Clark (1947), these theories have without warrant been applied to understanding ethnic identity development in general (for example, Phinney, 1993). Examination of ethnic identity development among other people of color is therefore necessary.

Also, as stated earlier, scholars have stressed the importance of middle childhood in discussing ethnic identity (for example, Hernandez Sheets, 1999; Spencer, 1985). However, in light of the belief that the adolescent experience involves a heightened sense of personal exploration, recent researchers have typically focused on adolescence. How can ethnic identity be defined and measured in younger populations?

Components of Ethnic Identity. Phinney (Phinney and Chavira, 1992; Phinney, 1996) lists several components of ethnic identity. Among them, the most fundamental component involves *ethnic identification*. Ethnic identification refers primarily to the awareness that a child belongs to an ethnic group represented by a label (Aboud, 1986). Bernal and her colleagues (1993) argue that ethnic identification represents a critical aspect in studying children's ethnic identity, since it is along this identification that children categorize themselves as belonging to certain groups, while recognizing that (1) common attributes are shared by the members and (2) there is a distinction between members of the group and others. Furthermore, children in middle childhood appear to attach affective and cognitive reactions to these labels (Rholes, Newman, and Ruble, 1990). Previous research on ethnic identity development, though almost exclusively based on African American and European American samples, appears to suggest that children begin to develop ethnic identification around three to four years of age (see for example, Weiland and Coughlin, 1979). Given recent changes in the demographics in the United States, inclusion of other children of color, especially those from immigrant backgrounds, is crucial in future studies addressing ethnic identification.

Measuring Ethnic Identification. Aboud (1986) suggests using ethnic labels primarily for examining the accuracy of identification; however, we contend that the potential utility of labels extends beyond accuracy assessment. First, the measure is inherently multidimensional, as children are asked to indicate whether each of a series of labels is about them; this is a step forward from the dilemma model discussed earlier. Naturally, researchers can tailor the list of labels, and it can concurrently contain not only ethnic labels but also others (gender, roles), so that each child's self-representation can be examined in a more "organic" way. In fact, Henry and Bankston (2001) assert that ethnic identity development may result from a "dialectical process involving internal and external opinions and processes as well as the individual's self-identification and outsiders' ethnic designations" (p. 1020); other researchers proceed further and promote inclusion of much wider dimensions, such as personality characteristics, gender, social role, religion, and so on (for example, Deaux, Reid, Mizrahi, and Ethier, 1995). Although the idea of viewing identity multidimensionally is not new, it has yet to be widely adopted. Most of the previous research has therefore defined, measured, and analyzed ethnic identity in a "social vacuum," that is, in isolation from other aspects of identity. This practice reflects a reductionistic tradition sometimes prevalent in the field of psychology (Ruble and others, 2004).

The second advantage associated with this measure is its flexibility, which allows further qualitative and quantitative explorations. For example, we suggest that, in order to measure priority among the labels and examine which are comparatively more important than others, children may rank-order the labels. In addition, to find out about the conceptualization of these labels, children may be asked to articulate the reasons for selecting a particular label. As shown, examining ethnic identification using labels may be developmentally appropriate for children in their middle childhood, and it allows a variety of issues (among them multiplicity, priority, and conceptualization) to be addressed. The main purpose of this study is to introduce a method of assessing identification which allows a variety of identification dimensions and populations to be included.

Method

Four hundred forty-eight children enrolled in first and fourth grades (mean age = 8.88, SD = 1.62; minimum age five, maximum twelve) were recruited to participate in the current study. The children were part of a larger cross-sectional longitudinal study; this cohort consisted of children with at least one parent from Portugal (n = 141), the Dominican Republic (n = 155) and Cambodia (n = 152). Children were divided into two age groups (first and fourth graders, mean age = 6.49, SD = .65 for the former and mean age = 9.46, SD = .66 for the latter). The sex and national backgrounds of the children were roughly equally distributed across various cells in this three (national background) by two (age group) by two (sex) design.

The Three Groups. The three immigrant groups in this study are among the largest local immigrant groups. Despite this commonality, there are noteworthy differences among the groups. For example, unlike Dominicans and the Portuguese, who have arrived primarily as voluntary labor migrants, the local Cambodian community arrived as refugees. Since the primary goal of the current study is to describe the normative trends of the development of ethnic group identification within each group, it does not necessarily follow the comparative framework whose primary focus is to highlight between-group differences. However, some of such analyses are inevitably informative on occasion and are therefore discussed when appropriate.

Multidimensional Measure of Identity. To target the issues of the development of ethnic identification among children in their middle childhood, a variation of a measure proposed collaboratively by Odette Alarcón, Sumru Erkut, and Cynthia García Coll (Alarcón, 1999) was developed. In this checklist-based method, children are presented with a list of identity labels. The current list consists of ninety-two words, generated through a series of pilot studies analyzing the cultural backgrounds of the students enrolled in twenty-one of the elementary schools among the schools where the study was conducted. The list was therefore exhaustive, so as to accommodate all children in the study. Clearly, the list can be tailored to accommodate any population being studied.

For administrative convenience, the list was separated into two tiers. The first consists of thirty-four labels that pertained to gender, role (son, student, and so on), and basic cultural markers including race (for example, white), ethnicity or panethnicity (Asian and others), religion (Catholic and so on), and some of their hyphenated derivatives, such as "Asian American," as well as three commonly used words referring to multiethnicity ("mixed," "biracial," and "half"). In short, these tier-one labels were either potentially applicable to all participants regardless of their racial or ethnic background or general labels to which children of all backgrounds were routinely exposed.

The second tier included fifty-eight specific nationality labels (for example, Chinese) and their hyphenated-American derivatives (for example, Dominican American), as defined by Portes and Rumbaut (1996). This tier included seventeen labels involving Asian panethnicity, nineteen Latino labels, and sixteen European labels, although each set included fillers that may not specifically be applicable to the current population (for example, German for the Portuguese). Ideally, all of these ninety-two words would be given to each individual. However, pilot testing revealed that inclusion of the entire list represented an excessive cognitive burden to elementary school children. Thus the list for each child consisted of only the tier-one words and an applicable subset of tier-two labels (that is, in addition to the tier-one words, Cambodian children were given only Asian-specific tier-two words). In the end, each child worked with a list of fifty-one (Cambodian), fifty-three (Dominican), or fifty (Portuguese) labels.

Interview Procedure. Children were interviewed individually, at school or at a public library, as a part of a larger three-year cross-sectional longitudinal project. Embedded within an extensive set of questions was the identification measure in question. At all locations, quiet work areas were provided. Interviewers were trained college and graduate students, matched for race and ethnicity with subjects. In the first phase of this task, each label on the list (described earlier) was read out to the child, and the child was asked to indicate whether or not it applied:

> Do you want to play a game? OK, here are the rules. I am going to read a list of words to you. For each one, I want you to tell me if it's about you or not. For example, if I say, "Are you a teacher?" and if you don't think you are a

teacher, then you'd say, "No." But if you think you are a teacher, then you'd say "Yes." I want you to think real hard because I don't want you to say, "Maybe." If I say words that you have never heard before or if you don't know what some of the words mean, probably those words aren't about you. Ready? Are you a _____

After completing this phase, we had the children rank-order the labels they selected. Given that the ability to mentally rank order does not develop until the age of nine or ten (Chapman and Lindenberger, 1988), each child was shown the labels she or he had chosen, individually written out on an index card, and the interviewer reviewed each label aloud. Then the interviewer asked which word was most important to the child. Interviewers set the selected card aside; the children were then asked to identify "the second most important" label. This routine was repeated for the remaining cards. They were allowed to revise their earlier choices at any time, while no ties were allowed. Perhaps due to its concrete, gamelike properties, these children were able to prioritize their identity labels with ease. Then, for each label, we asked, "Tell me, why is [label] about you?" in order to examine their construction of these labels. Throughout this task, interviewers stressed that it was acceptable, but not necessary, to repeat the same answers, and that there were no right or wrong reasons.

Results and Discussion

The children selected, on average, 7.1 labels ($SD = 2.3$; range = 2 to 16). There was no significant difference in the number of labels selected on the basis of gender, but there were main effects for both age and national backgrounds. Specifically, older children chose significantly more labels than did younger children ($M = 7.7$, $SD = 2.0$ and $M = 6.6$, $SD = 2.4$, respectively; $t = 5.1$, $p < .001$) and Dominican children chose significantly more labels ($M = 8.1$, $SD = 2.5$) than did either Portuguese ($M = 6.7$, $SD = 1.9$) or Cambodian children ($M = 6.5$, $SD = 1.9$; $F(2, 429) = 27.5$, $p < .001$). All of the children chose a gender descriptor and at least one ethnicity label, and 77 percent also chose a family role (for example, child or daughter), in contrast with only 36 percent who chose a racial label (such as black) and 26 percent who chose a religious descriptor (for instance, Christian).

Racial and Ethnic Descriptors. It is critical to note that the main effect due to national backgrounds in the number of labels children selected is linked to the number of labels presented to them (fifty-one for Cambodians, fifty-three for Dominicans, and fifty for the Portuguese) and the pool of labels that objectively describe them. Subsequent analyses therefore focus primarily on within-group variability, and between-group analyses are conducted while controlling for the differences in the number of available labels.

Characteristics Within Each Group. Within each immigrant group, there were no differences in the number of ethnic labels that were based on gender, but there were significant differences on the basis of age. The older children (Ms = 4.2, 4.2, 2.0; SDs = 1.1, 1.9, .59, for Cambodians, Dominicans, and Portuguese) in each group chose a significantly greater number of labels than did the younger children (Ms = .98, 3.0, 1.4; SDs = .53, 1.5, .71, for Cambodians, Dominicans, and Portuguese; ts = 10.5, 4.1, and 5.2, respectively; all ps < .001).

Which ethnic or racial labels did these children select? Among the Cambodian children, the most commonly chosen ethnic label was "Cambodian," which was chosen by 95 percent of the younger cohort and 99 percent of the older cohort. This was followed by "Khmer," which, though chosen by 79 percent of the younger cohort, was chosen by significantly more of the older cohort, 97 percent ($\chi^2_{(df=1)}$ = 12.4, p < .001). The word *Khmer* is a comprehensive and abstract Cambodian term that is inclusive not only of the language but also of the people and the religion of Cambodia. As such, it is not surprising that older children were more aware of this term than were their younger counterparts.

The significant difference on the basis of age is also reflected in the choice of the terms *Cambodian American* (37 percent of the younger cohort and 73 percent of the older cohort, [$\chi^2_{(df=1)}$ = 19.6, p < .001]), *Asian* (17 percent of the younger cohort and 87 percent of the older cohort, [$\chi^2_{(df=1)}$ = 72.2, p < .001]), and *Asian American* (12 percent of the younger cohort and 57 percent of the older cohort, [$\chi^2_{(df=1)}$ = 34.0, p < .001]). These trends suggest that fourth graders, compared to their counterparts in the first grade, were more aware of a wider variety of racial and ethnic labels that applied to them.

Parallel to the Cambodians, among the Dominican children the most commonly chosen ethnic label was "Dominican," favored by 87 percent of the younger cohort and 95 percent of the older cohort, though there was no significant difference due to age. The second most frequently cited label was "Spanish" (85 percent of the younger cohort and 89 percent of the older cohort), and then "Spanish American" (34 percent of the younger cohort and 37 percent of the older cohort). The least common label was "Latina/Latino," with only 11 percent of the younger cohort and 35 percent of the older cohort ($\chi^2_{(df=1)}$ = 12.0, p < .001), indicating that this panethnic label was not commonly understood by children in their middle childhood, particularly the first graders.

Among the Portuguese children, the predominant selection was "Portuguese," chosen by 87 percent of the younger children and 99 percent of the older children ($\chi^2_{(df=1)}$ = 6.96, p < .01), followed by "Portuguese American" with 48 percent of the younger children and 83 percent of the older children ($\chi^2_{(df=1)}$ = 18.2, p < .001). Extremely few children chose "Azorean" (one girl from the younger cohort and seven boys from the older cohort) or "Azorean American" (three children from the younger cohort and six from the older cohort). This is noteworthy because the Portuguese children in the current study were decidedly of Azorean descent, and hence these labels theoretically applied to these children. The current results, however, indicate that the Azorean identification did not play a major role in these children's descriptions of themselves. This is consistent with Waters's notion (1996) of optional identity—that it is only an option for "white" children to identify with and explore their Azorean backgrounds, because these children are in a society in which theirs is the race in power and there exists little urgency to establish themselves racially (Aboud, 1986). Developmentally, therefore, it is plausible that their Azorean background may be incorporated in the self-definitions of our Portuguese sample later on.

Across all three groups, the most popular choices are the nationally based descriptor (Cambodian, Dominican, Portuguese), which become more pronounced with age. The second most popular choices are culturally based, with Khmer and Spanish. This trend did not apply to the Portuguese children here; it is fair to state, though, that children in all groups tended to describe themselves primarily along their national and cultural backgrounds. The least popular choices are panethnically based, such as Asian; this makes sense because panethnicity, according to Lopez and Espiritu (1990), is a socially constructed grouping that categorizes people who have little in common yet are perceived to belong together in mainstream American society. With age and increased exposure to the discourse of race and ethnicity in the United States, these children appear to come to understand that a range of labels apply, including those not inherently meaningful to them.

Salience of Identification: Prevalence and Priority. As an indicator of the salience of ethnic identity dimensions, we would like to consider two relevant concepts: *prevalence* and *priority*. Prevalence is the proportion of ethnic or racial labels chosen out of the total number of labels selected. In this exploratory study, we had unequal numbers of labels applicable to each immigrant group; hence, we can only tentatively discuss group differences. Across the three groups of younger children, the Dominican children chose a significantly larger proportion of their ethnic or racial labels ($M = .43$, $SD = .21$) than did either the Cambodians ($M = .35$, $SD = .14$) or the Portuguese ($M = .35$, $SD = .18$, $F_{(2, 207)} = 5.4$, $p < .01$). However, across the three groups of older children, Dominican ($M = .59$, $SD = .23$) and Cambodian children ($M = .61$, $SD = .16$) both selected a higher proportion of ethnic or racial labels than their Portuguese counterparts ($M = .50$, $SD = .15$, $F_{(2, 218)} = 7.0$, $p < .001$).

Although prevalence is a clear-cut way of conceptualizing ethnic identity, scholars may wish to consider the relative importance among identity dimensions, or *priority*. Among both the Cambodian and the Dominican children, the most important construct was that of ethnicity (45 percent and 46 percent respectively), followed closely by gender (34 percent and 27 percent respectively), with no significant differences according to gender or age for either group. Among the Portuguese children, there is an opposite ordering such that the most important construct was that of gender (45 percent), followed closely by ethnicity (26 percent), with no significant differences by gender or age. For both Cambodian and Dominican children, ethnicity was the most important in contrast to gender for the Portuguese children ($\chi^2_{(df=12)} = 23.5$, $p < .05$). This validates the assumption that ethnicity may be salient to children of color, while gender represents the primary social identity for European American children (Aboud, 1986).

Although not suitable for the current data set, which includes unequal numbers of labels across groups and across dimensions, we would like to demonstrate how the current method may be used to quantify the priority among identity dimensions. If researchers were to include a single descriptor for each aspect of identity (such as gender, race, family role, religion, and so forth; one may also include other dimensions such as personality and physical characteristics), they could weigh each label by its rank order. For example, Table 3.1 depicts the case of two hypothetical children who selected four identical labels, but in different orders. Although these two children have the same *prevalence* along each dimension, Child A clearly assigns greater importance to her gender, family role, and religion than she does to her ethnicity (nationality), while Child B regards his ethnicity as paramount. A mathematical formula may allow us to numerically represent such situations. In so doing, one can assign the reverse of the obtained rank orders to determine a factored placement score (FPS). The FPS for each identity aspect is computed as the number corresponding to the reverse of the obtained rank order divided by the total number of labels selected. Thus, the FPS for each of the descriptors for Child A and Child B is indicated in Table 3.1.

Thus we could quantify the relative importance of each dimension of each child's ethnicity. Child A would have a value of .1 for her ethnicity, while Child B would have .4; by contrast, gender represents a value of .4 for Child A while it is only .1 for Child B. Hence, in discussing the strength of ethnic identification, it may be useful to consider priority in addition to prevalence. As seen, both prevalence and priority allow parametric statistical analysis, and they could produce different results; future research should take advantage of such a tool.

Table 3.1. Calculating Factor Placement Scores (FPS)

	Child A				Child B		
Choice	Label	Rank	Reverse	Factor Placement Score	Label	Rank	Reverse	Factor Placement Score
1	Girl	1	4	.40	Dominican	1	4	.40
2	Daughter	2	3	.30	Christian	2	3	.30
3	Christian	3	2	.20	Daughter	3	2	.20
4	Dominican	4	1	.10	Girl	4	1	.10

Conceptualization of Identity Dimensions

To analyze the reasons given for each label, the responses were independently coded by two raters, with a Cohen's kappa of 93. A third rater reconciled discrepancies. In general, the children's responses ranged from concrete ideas such as physical traits ("I am white because my skin is white"), nativity or geography ("I was born here"), and linguistic abilities ("I speak Spanish"); relational ideas such as their families' heritage ("My mom is Portuguese"); and valence-attached reactions ("I am a girl because boys are bad"). Other responses revealed socially defined expectations ("I am a girl because I get to wear dresses and fix my hair"). The breadth of responses clearly signals that these questions elicited a variety of notions reflecting notable variability not only across children but also across labels.

Even though children were fairly adept at providing adultlike explanations for their social group memberships in general, this proved to be a somewhat challenging task, particularly for the first graders, as evidenced by answers of "I don't know," answers that simply repeated the label "Because I am," and answers that were nonsequiturs ("I am Catholic because I can jump high"). For the most important label, 21 percent of the children did not know why, 13 percent repeated the label, and 4 percent gave nonsequiturs; in other words, 38 percent failed to give informative answers. Specifically, 63 percent of the younger cohort responded with "I don't know" for their first chosen label, in contrast to 37 percent of the older cohort ($\chi^2_{(df=20)}$ = 20.5, $p < .01$), and significantly more Cambodians (43 percent) responded with not knowing as compared with the Portuguese (33 percent) and Dominicans (23 percent, $\chi^2_{(df=40)}$ = 30, $p < .05$). When affective reactions were evident in their answers, most children simply expressed happiness at being what they were ("I am happy to be Dominican"). It is notable, though, that such responses occurred exclusively among the first graders (7 percent for younger, 0 percent for older).

Not surprisingly, the reasons for the labels were inextricably linked with what they were trying to explain, and there were age differences (see Table 3.2). When an ethnic label was chosen as most important, the younger children's ($n = 82$) most often cited reason was "I don't know" (31 percent), followed by the linguistic characteristics of the children and their families (22 percent) and then nativity (12 percent). Among the older children who chose an ethnic label first ($n = 88$), 30 percent cited nativity, 25 percent noted their family's heritage, and 17 percent mentioned linguistic characteristics, while only 11 percent responded "I don't know." It should be noted that these are largely adultlike explanations for the ethnic identifiers, and the range of responses here suggests the inherently multidimensional nature of these ethnic group labels. Under these circumstances, it is reasonable to conclude that older children were less likely to articulate uncritical valuation of their own ethnic groups or devaluation of other ethnic groups.

Table 3.2. Predominant Explanations for Children's Most Important Identity Label

	Gender	Ethnicity	Family Role	Religion
Don't know				
Younger	.29	.31	.13	.19
Older	.15	.11	.22	.21
Repeat label				
Younger	.23	.07	.13	.00
Older	.21	.03	.19	.00
Physical traits				
Younger	.26	.02	.13	.00
Older	.28	.00	.11	.00
Nativity/geography				
Younger	.00	.12	.00	.00
Older	.00	.30	.00	.00
Family heritage				
Younger	.00	.07	.00	.06
Older	.00	.25	.00	.00
Language				
Younger	.00	.22	.00	.00
Older	.00	.17	.00	.00
Beliefs/attitudes				
Younger	.03	.03	.25	.37
Older	.08	.00	.40	.57
Positive affect				
Younger	.03	.07	.00	.06
Older	.01	.00	.00	.07

It is interesting to note that the children in our current sample appeared to have an easier time explaining the basis of their ethnic or racial group membership than gender group membership; this further supports the view that the children demonstrated a rather sophisticated understanding of these cultural labels as preadolescents. Overall, gender labels were more likely to produce a response of "I don't know" or simply repeating the label (52 percent for younger, 36 percent for older) than for ethnicity (38 percent for younger, 14 percent for older), family role (26 percent for younger, 41 percent for older), or religion (19 percent for younger, 21 percent for older). These results conflict with previous research (for example, Ramsey, 1991) indicating that children's awareness of their gender group affiliation develop somewhat earlier than their ethnic or racial group affiliation. It is feasible that children of color from immigrant backgrounds have a more "advanced" understanding of their ethnic background than of their gender, because of the salience of ethnicity for these children (Akiba and García Coll, 2003).

Conclusion

This chapter has focused on the importance of viewing ethnic identity as a multidimensional—as opposed to singular—concept, which deserves to be studied within the context of other identity dimensions. The preliminary analyses of the data, based on first and fourth graders from immigrant families, support such a view. For example, each child in all three groups selected a variety of labels, although labels referring to nationality (for example, Dominican) proved to be among the most commonly selected ones. Hence the current approach afforded us a wider picture of a child's ethnic identification, as we focused beyond the accuracy or strength of ethnic identity along singular dimensions. In addition, children willingly prioritized and justified these labels, further suggesting the multifaceted nature of their definitions of self. This signals that their identification is frequently accompanied by knowledge of the essential characteristics that aligned them with others in a particular social group and set its members apart from members of other groups. Given the evident ease and diagnosticity associated with this identification measure in the current population, its usefulness in understanding the personal and social identification among U.S.-born children of color is potentially enormous.

Further analyses on prevalence, priority, and reasoning behind selection of the labels may also allow researchers to create "profiles" of each child's ethnic identity within the context of other identity dimensions, while considering the interactions among these labels. For example, selecting "girl" as the top label as an African American child may be qualitatively and conceptually different from selecting the same label as a European American child, since the construals and consequences of gender identity frequently vary with the culture (hooks, 1985). Thus concluding that an African American girl and a European American girl equally value their gender highly, though factually correct, may require further qualification, given the potential variability in their conceptualizations of gender. Follow-up questions, such as the one used in the current study, may thus be a crucial tool to put our quantitative findings in context. Although the study presented here included only a limited set of social group categories and role labels, this measure can be expanded to include other personal and social identity dimensions. We are in the process of using these profiles as correlates of other processes and variables, such as attitude toward school, school performance, and routine ethnic practices at home among the children in the current study. Future endeavors should focus on establishing the validity of the measure proposed in this study, while exploring its predictive utilities.

References

Aboud, F. E. "The Development of Ethnic Self-Identification and Attitudes." In J. S. Phinney and M. J. Rotheram (eds.), *Children's Ethnic Socialization*. Thousand Oaks, Calif.: Sage, 1986.

Akiba, D., and García Coll, C. T. "Effective Interventions with Children of Color and Their Families: A Contextual, Developmental Approach." In T. Smith (ed.), *Affirming Diversity: Practicing Multiculturalism in Counseling and Psychology.* Needham Heights, Mass.: Allyn & Bacon, 2003.

Alarcón, O. "Ethnic Identity of Puerto Rican Children Raised in the Mainland." Paper presented at the biennial meeting of the Society for Research on Child Development, Albuquerque, N.M., Apr. 15–18, 1999.

Bernal, M. E., and others. "Development of Mexican American Identity." In M. E. Bernal and G. P. Knight (eds.), *Ethnic Identity: Formation and Transmission Among Hispanic and Other Minorities.* Albany: State University of New York Press, 1993.

Branch, C. "Race and Human Development." In R. Hernandez-Sheets and E. R. Hollins (eds.), *Racial and Ethnic Identity in School Practices.* Mahwah, N.J.: Erlbaum, 1999.

Branch, C., and Newcombe, N. "A Longitudinal and Cross-Sectional Study of the Development of Racial Attitudes of Black Children as a Function of Parental Attitudes." *Child Development,* 1986, *57,* 712–721.

Chapman, M., and Lindenberger, U. "Functions, Operations, and Decalage in the Development of Transitivity." *Developmental Psychology,* 1988, *24,* 542–551.

Clark, K. B., and Clark, M. P. "The Development of Consciousness of Self and the Emergence of Racial Identification in Negro Pre-School Children." *Journal of Social Psychology,* 1939, *10,* 591–599.

Clark, K. B., and Clark, M. P. "Racial Identification and Preference in Negro Children." In T. M. Newcomb and E. L. Hartley (eds.), *Readings in Social Psychology.* New York: Holt, 1947.

Cross, W. E. "Negro-to-Black Conversion Experience." *Black World,* 1971, *20,* 13–27.

Cross, W. E. *Shades of Black: Diversity in African-American Identity.* Philadelphia: Temple University Press, 1991.

Cross, W. E., Parham, T. A., and Helms, J. E. "Negrescence Revisited: Theory and Research." In R. L. Jones (ed.), *African-American Identity Development.* Hampton, Va.: Cobb & Henry Publishers, 1998.

Damon, W., and Hart, D. *Self-Understanding in Childhood and Adolescence.* New York: Cambridge University Press, 1988.

Deaux, K., Reid, A., Mizrahi, K., and Ethier, K. A. "Parameters of Social Identity." *Journal of Personality and Social Psychology,* 1995, *68,* 280–291.

Eder, R. A. "The Emergent Personologist: The Structure and Content of $3\frac{1}{2}$-, $5\frac{1}{2}$-, and $7\frac{1}{2}$-Year Olds' Concepts of Themselves and Other Persons." *Child Development,* 1989, *60,* 1218–1228.

Erikson, E. H. *Identity: Youth and Crisis.* New York: Norton, 1968.

Gibbs, J. T., and Huang, L. N. "A Conceptual Framework for Assessing and Treating Minority Youth." In J. T. Gibbs and L. N. Huang (eds.), *Children of Color: Psychological Interventions with Minority Youth.* San Francisco: Jossey-Bass, 1989.

Harter, S. "Developmental Changes in Self-Understanding Across the 5 to 7 Shift." In A. J. Sameroff and M. M. Haith (eds.), *The Five to Seven Year Shift.* Chicago: University of Chicago Press, 1996.

Helms, J. E. "Toward a Theoretical Explanation of the Effects of Race on Counseling: A Black and White Model." *Counseling Psychologist,* 1984, *12,* 153–165.

Henry, J. M., and Bankston, C. L. "Ethnic Self-Identification and Symbolic Stereotyping: The Portrayal of Louisiana Cajuns." *Ethnic and Racial Studies,* 2001, *24,* 1020–1045.

Hernandez Sheets, R. "Human Development and Ethnic Identity." In R. Hernandez Sheets and E. R. Hollins (eds.), *Racial and Ethnic Identity in School Practices*. Mahwah, N.J.: Erlbaum, 1999.
hooks, b. *Ain't I a Woman: Black Women and Feminism*. Boston: South End Press, 1985.
Horowitz, R. "Racial Aspects of Self-Identification in Nursery School Children." *Journal of Psychology*, 1939, 7, 91–99.
Lopez, D., and Espiritu, Y. "Panethnicity in the United States: A Theoretical Framework." *Ethnic and Racial Studies*, 1990, 13, 198–224.
Marcia, J. E. "Identity in Adolescence." In J. Adelson (ed.), *Handbook of Adolescent Psychology*. New York: Wiley, 1980.
McLoyd, V. "Conceptual and Methodological Issues in the Study of Ethnic Minority Children and Adolescents." In H. E. Fitzgerald, B. M. Lexter, and B. S. Zuckerman (eds.), *Children of Color: Research, Health and Policy Issues*. New York: Garland, 1999.
Phinney, J. S. "Stages of Ethnic Identity Development in Minority Group Adolescents." *Journal of Early Adolescence*, 1989, 9, 34–49.
Phinney, J. S. "A Three-Stage Model of Ethnic Identity Development in Adolescence." In M. E. Bernal and G. P. Knight (eds.), *Ethnic Identity: Formation and Transmission Among Hispanic and Other Minorities*. Albany: State University of New York Press, 1993.
Phinney, J. S. "When We Talk About American Ethnic Groups, What Do We Mean?" *American Psychologist*, 1996, 51, 918–926.
Phinney, J. S., and Chavira, V. "Ethnic Identity and Self-Esteem: An Exploratory Longitudinal Study." *Journal of Adolescence*, 1992, 15, 271–281.
Portes, A., and Rumbaut, R. G. *Immigrant America: A Portrait*. Berkeley: University of California Press, 1996.
Ramsey, P. G. "The Salience of Race in Young Children Growing Up in All-White Community." *Journal of Educational Psychology*, 1991, 83, 28–34.
Rholes, W. S., Newman, L. S., and Ruble, D. N. "Understanding Self and Other: Developmental and Motivational Aspects of Perceiving Persons in Terms of Invariant Dispositions." In E. T. Higgins and R. M. Sorrentino (Eds.), *Handbook of Motivation and Cognition: Foundations of Social Behavior, Volume 2*. New York: Guilford Press, 1990.
Ruble, D. N., and others. "The Development of a Sense of a 'We': The Emergence and Implications of Children's Collective Identity." In M. Bennett and F. Sani (eds.), *The Development of the Social Self*. East Sussex, England: Psychology Press, 2004.
Spencer, M. B. "Cultural Cognition and Social Cognition as Identity Factors in Black Children's Personal Growth." In M. Spencer, G. Brookings, and W. Allen (eds.), *Beginnings: The Social and Affective Development of Black Children*. Mahwah, N.J.: Erlbaum, 1985.
Suarez-Orozco, C., & Suarez-Orozco, M. M. *Children of Immigration*. Cambridge, Mass.: Harvard University Press. 2002.
Szkrybalo, J., and Ruble, D. N. "'God Made Me a Girl': Sex-Category Consistency Judgments and Explanations Revised." *Developmental Psychology*, 1999, 35, 392–402.
Waters, M. C. "Optional Ethnicities: For Whites Only?" In S. Pedraza and R. G. Rumbaut (eds.), *Origins and Destinies: Immigration, Race and Ethnicity in America*. Belmont, Calif.: Wadsworth, 1996.
Weiland, A., and Coughlin, R. "Self-Identification and Preferences: A Comparison of White and Mexican American First and Third Graders." *Journal of Cross-Cultural Psychology*, 1979, 10, 356–365.

Daisuke Akiba is assistant professor of educational psychology at City University of New York's Queens College and the Graduate School and University Center in New York City.

Laura A. Szalacha is visiting assistant professor of human development and education at Brown University in Providence, Rhode Island.

Cynthia T. García Coll is Charles Pitts Robinson and John Palmer Barstow Professor of education, psychology, and pediatrics at Brown University in Providence, Rhode Island, and the Mittleman Family Director of the Center for the Study of Human Development at the university.

4

The complexities of autonomy and connectedness in the self-conceptions of late adolescent European Americans provide empirical support for the theoretical position that autonomy and connectedness are multifaceted and interrelated self-characteristics that reflect cultural values about individuals in relation to others.

Within-Culture Complexities: Multifaceted and Interrelated Autonomy and Connectedness Characteristics in Late Adolescent Selves

Catherine Raeff

Since the 1980s, it has become commonplace for developmentalists to invoke issues of independence and interdependence as a way to describe and explain cultural differences in varied aspects of development. During this time, the view that the United States and all things European American are essentially independence-oriented while the non-Western world is essentially interdependence-oriented has become deeply ingrained and pervasive, almost taking on the status of an inviolate assumption. However, elaborating on some dissenting voices that have emerged over the years, this volume makes clear that characterizing cultures in such unidimensional terms obscures the complexities of cultural processes, as well as self-development. Thus, the assumption is being questioned, and a theoretical shift is occurring in an effort to conceptualize the complexities of co-occurring aspects of autonomy and connectedness.

Dichotomous Conceptualizations of Autonomy and Connectedness

When developmental psychologists first became captivated by autonomy and connectedness in the 1980s, these constructs were typically conceptualized as dichotomous dimensions of human behavior, development, and

I am grateful to the study participants, and I thank Julie Shrager and Danielle Swoboda for their research assistance.

culture (Raeff, forthcoming). This dichotomous perspective holds that self-development within a culture follows either an autonomy trajectory or a connectedness trajectory, but not both (Markus and Kitayama, 1991; Sampson, 1977; Triandis, 1995). Within this view, the generally Western, and specifically European American, cultural goals of self-development are defined in terms of separation and disengagement from others. Thus, self-development for European Americans has been characterized in terms of independence, whereby people from childhood through adulthood are said to conceptualize themselves primarily as autonomous individuals. Such individuals are assumed to pursue individual goals, with little if any regard for the importance of relationships in establishing and maintaining the self.

For example, Sampson (1977) describes European American culture in terms of valuing the self-contained individual, further pointing out that "the self-contained person is one who does not require or desire others for his or her completion in life; self-contained persons either are or hope to be entire unto themselves. Self-containment is the extreme of independence: needing or wanting no one. It is fundamentally antithetical to the concept of interdependence" (p. 770).

It is also claimed that this view of the self remains strong among Americans in the twenty-first century because they conceptualize themselves as essentially self-made people whose development is relatively unaffected by relationships (Sampson, 2000). This argument is partly based on a *New York Times Magazine* survey (May 7, 2000) indicating a high rate of agreement (85 percent) with the statement "I believe it is possible in America to pretty much be who [sic] you want to be." However, this survey item is a rather broad statement that could be interpreted in various ways that do not necessarily involve viewing oneself as self-made. For example, it can be interpreted as reflecting an American ideal that all people are free to at least think up and try to pursue any imaginable dream, or as reflecting the fact that in the United States there are no legal restrictions associated with economic background regarding who can pursue varied occupations. Furthermore, it is unclear why the survey did not include items about more direct social connections, such as family relationships and friends. Moreover, asking people to rate certain social factors that are preconceived by an investigator does not provide much information about their subjective understandings of their own development. Thus it may also prove informative to ask a more open-ended question, such as, "How did you get to be the way you are today?"

In keeping with a dichotomous view of autonomy and connectedness, Markus and Kitayama (1991) also claim that within an independence orientation the self is seen "as an independent, self-contained, autonomous entity" (p. 224). This kind of autonomous self is alleged to stand in stark contrast to the self that develops within interdependence-oriented cultures. Apparently, from the point of view of an interdependent self, an autonomous self would represent "a bizarre idea cutting the self off from the interdependent whole,

WITHIN-CULTURE COMPLEXITIES   63

dooming it to a life of isolation and loneliness" (Shweder and Bourne, 1984, p. 194).

Although it has provided some important information, this dichotomous perspective remains limited because it undermines the position that human beings are by nature, or at least from birth on, physically and mentally separate, and simultaneously socially connected. Certainly, it has not been disputed that human infants the world over require social connections for survival, and a multitude of infancy studies shows that human infants are predisposed to be active social partners and pupils (Užgiris, 1989). Human infants are also prepared for independent functioning as they are able to engage in organized sensorimotor activities that enable them to begin acting on the world, and construing their experiences as mentally separate individuals (Piaget, 1953). Building on these foundations during development, people remain mentally and physically separate, and simultaneously connected to others through varied relationships and social roles. In terms of self-development, there is increasing empirical evidence to support the view that both autonomy and connectedness are important aspects of the self in varied cultural contexts (see Mines, 1988; Offer, Ostrov, Howard, and Atkinson, 1988; Rosenberger, 1992; Spiro, 1993). Moreover, studies with European American children and adolescents point to the importance of defining oneself not only as a separate person with individual needs and goals but also in relation to specific others, and in terms of wider social roles (Damon and Hart, 1988; Harter, 1999; Offer, Ostrov, Howard, and Atkinson, 1988; Steinberg and Silverberg, 1986). Overall, a meta-analysis of studies that are informed by a dichotomous approach to autonomy and connectedness indicates that cultures and selves cannot be clearly differentiated according to this one dimension, and that a dichotomous approach obscures complex cultural and self processes (Oyserman, Coon, and Kemmelmeier, 2002).

In keeping with the position that autonomy and connectedness are basic to the human condition and given the empirical evidence regarding the complexities of human functioning and self-conceptualization, dichotomous conceptions of autonomy and connectedness are now slowly being replaced by theoretical conceptions of autonomy and connectedness as co-occurring dimensions of self that are shaped by cultural values (Grotevant and Cooper, 1998; Guisinger and Blatt, 1994; Turiel, 1996). Although it is gaining ground, a co-occurrence position still requires some refinement and obliges us to address at least two basic, interrelated theoretical questions: (1) How can autonomy and connectedness be conceptualized? and (2) What is the nature of co-occurrence between autonomy and connectedness?

My goal in this chapter is to offer some answers to these questions by presenting a theoretical approach to issues of autonomy and connectedness in relation to the self. Qualitative, empirical illustrations of this theoretical approach from a study of European American late adolescents' self-conceptions will also be presented. I certainly realize that this study includes just one cultural group, and a cultural group that has been rather overrepresented in developmental psychology research. Nevertheless, it is important to continue studying this cultural group because it has routinely been characterized in terms of autonomy. Thus European American self-conceptions can be a good test case for the current approach to autonomy and connectedness as co-occurring aspects of the self. Moreover, this study can also provide information about previously neglected aspects of connectedness among European Americans.

Reconceptualizing Autonomy and Connectedness in Relation to the Self

The current theoretical approach to autonomy and connectedness in relation to self-development is partly derived from varied established perspectives on the self. In particular, I acknowledge that my thinking about this issue has been largely shaped by Western perspectives on the self, especially the theoretical traditions of William James, George Herbert Mead, and Erik Erikson. It is interesting that, in keeping with a dichotomous approach to autonomy and connectedness, it has been commonplace to characterize Western psychological traditions as independence-oriented, or focused on autonomy (see Markus and Kitayama, 1994; Sampson, 1989). Although Western psychology has generally focused on the individual, varied theories in Western psychology have actually long pointed to the importance of both autonomy and connectedness for human functioning. Indeed, social factors are central to James's theory of the self, and both direct social relationships and wider societal concerns are central to Mead's and Erikson's theories of the self.

In distinguishing between the self as subject and the self as object, James (1983) divided the self into the now-well-known I and Me, and his discussion of these self constituents points to the multifaceted nature of the self. Using Damon and Hart's more recent terminology (1988), the Me consists of physical, social, psychological, and active constituents. According to James, the "social self is the recognition which [one] gets from others" (p. 281), and James considers such social recognition to be virtually life sustaining. In addition, social factors not only constitute a constituent of the self, but they may also be part of other self constituents. For example, James explains that the physical Me consists of family members who are integral to the self because they are "bone of our bone and flesh of our flesh. When they die, a part of our very selves is gone. If they do anything wrong, it is our shame. If they are insulted, our anger flashes forth as readily as if we stood in their place" (p. 280). Moreover, each of the Me constituents may take on several dimensions, further revealing the multifaceted nature of the self. For example, multifaceted physical dimensions of the self include not only direct relationships but also one's body and material possessions.

Like James, Mead's approach to the self (1962) is inseparable from his association with the American philosophy of pragmatism, which holds that humans are active and social beings whose behavior serves and reflects social functioning (Odin, 1996). Within this social framework, Mead offers a thoroughly social conceptualization of the Me self as the process by which a person views his or her own behavior from the perspective of others during the course of interpersonal interactions. With development, the varied attitudes of others are then integrated and internalized in the form of the "generalized other," which represents the attitudes of the wider society to which a person belongs. According to Mead, "The organized community or social group which gives to the individual his unity of self may be called the 'generalized other'" (1962, p. 154).

At the same time that Mead conceptualizes the self in relation to wider societal connections and direct social interactions, he also points to the importance of an individual's autonomy in the form of the I self. The I is the part of the self that enables an individual to interpret and react to wider societal attitudes in his or her own unique way, which in turn enables the individual to contribute to the very construction of societal attitudes. Thus "there is always a mutual relationship of the individual and the community in which the individual lives" (Mead, 1962, p. 216), so that varied dimensions of autonomy and connectedness are inseparably engaged in an ongoing intersection (Marková, 2000).

Although I question the psychoanalytic basis of Erikson's theory of identity formation (1980), his view of the self, or identity, has much to offer, especially as one of the few lifespan developmental approaches to self-development. His theory is clearly different from Mead's, but like Mead Erikson is concerned with how identity formation is socially constituted. Erikson also conceptualizes identity in terms of inseparable aspects of autonomy and connectedness (Grotevant and Cooper, 1998; Guisinger and Blatt, 1994; Josselson, 1994), as his posited eight stages of identity formation involve defining oneself both as a separate individual and in relation to others. According to Erikson, forming such an identity involves "the immediate perception of one's selfsameness and continuity in time; and the simultaneous perception of the fact that others recognize one's sameness and continuity" (1980, p. 22). In this way, recognizing oneself may be viewed as an aspect of autonomy that is inseparable from recognition by others. Ultimately, a person finds "a niche in some section of his society, a niche which is firmly defined and yet seems to be uniquely made for him" (p. 120). This kind of societal niche enables a person to express his or her individuality by contributing to society in his or her own unique way (Waterman, 1992). Again, we see that autonomy and connectedness are inseparable, or interrelated, since there is an ongoing interplay between individual and societal functioning.

Although James, Mead, and Erikson offer very different approaches to the self, we may take two key points from this brief overview of their theories. First, the self is a system that consists of multifaceted constituents, which themselves may be multifaceted. Second, autonomy and connectedness are inseparable or interrelated aspects of the self. Building on these varied foundational approaches, we may now answer our two basic theoretical questions regarding autonomy, connectedness, and the self. To answer our first question (How can autonomy and connectedness be conceptualized?), autonomy and connectedness may be conceptualized as multifaceted dimensions of the self. That is, a person may conceptualize himself or herself as autonomous in varied ways, and a person may conceptualize himself or herself in terms of varied modes of connectedness. For example, some multifaceted autonomy self-characteristics may involve viewing oneself as a mentally separate being, as self-reliant, and as self-confident. Some multifaceted connectedness self characteristics may involve conceptualizing oneself in relation to specific others, in relation to wider societal concerns, and in terms of social activities.

To answer our second theoretical question (What is the nature of co-occurrence between autonomy and connectedness?), some dimensions of autonomy and connectedness co-occur as interrelated or inseparable dimensions of the self. For example, finding self-fulfillment may be a developing form of autonomy, but for some people self-fulfillment may be achieved only through maintaining satisfying relationships with others. Or a person may claim to be self-confident, and further probing may reveal that being self-confident means feeling comfortable with other people.

My approach to autonomy, connectedness, and the self is also derived from the theoretical view that human functioning and development are culturally situated. Within this view, varied aspects of human functioning reflect a complex and dynamic system of cultural meanings and values about human behavior and being. Specifically regarding the self, multifaceted and interrelated dimensions of autonomy and connectedness are taken to be constructed differently in varied cultural contexts, in relation to a particular culture's system of meanings and values regarding independent and social functioning.

The Current Study

The current theoretical approach has several implications that informed the current empirical study. First, this approach implies that people, including adolescents, conceptualize themselves as both autonomous and connected to others. Moreover, their conceptions of themselves as autonomous and connected are multifaceted; that is, there is more than one way to conceptualize oneself as autonomous and connected to others. Second, this approach implies that people's conceptions of themselves involve some interrelated or inseparable dimensions of autonomy and connectedness. That is, some stated self-characteristics are not classifiable exclusively in terms of autonomy or connectedness, but both. Finally, this approach implies that people's self-conceptions as autonomous and socially connected reflect cultural values about optimal modes of independent and social functioning.

To investigate these implications of the current theoretical approach to autonomy and connectedness in relation to the self, a study of late adolescent self-conceptualization was conducted. This study consisted of thirty-six European American eighteen-to-twenty-one-year-olds (nineteen males, seventeen females) from middle and low socioeconomic backgrounds. The participants' parents' educational achievement was used as the main marker of socioeconomic background, and eighteen participants had parents who completed high school or vocational training. For the other eighteen participants, fifteen had parents with at least a bachelor's degree, and three had at least one parent with a bachelor's degree and one parent who had attended some college without earning a degree.

Semistructured self-concept interviews were conducted with the participants. For the current discussion, we consider the participants' self characteristics, elicited by the general question, "Tell me about yourself; who are you; how would you describe yourself?" To enhance understanding of the participants' subjective self-constructions, they were then asked to explain why their varied self-characteristics are important. If necessary, further probes ("Why?" "How come?" "What do you mean?") were used to clarify the participants' ideas. In an effort to address some of the issues discussed earlier regarding the claim that Americans view themselves as self-made, we also consider the participants' answers to the question, "How did you get to be the way you are today?"

Results and Discussion

When asked to describe themselves in general, the participants discussed a mean of 5.92 (SD = 1.96) characteristics. The varied coding categories for connectedness, autonomy, and interrelated autonomy and connectedness self-characteristics will be presented later in this section. Overall, thirty-five (97 percent) of the thirty-six participants discussed at least one interrelated autonomy and connectedness characteristic; thirty-three (92 percent) discussed at least one connectedness characteristic, and twenty-three (64 percent) discussed at least one autonomy characteristic. A mean of 41 percent (SD = .21) of the participants' statements consisted of connectedness characteristics; a mean of 36 percent (SD = .22) consisted of interrelated autonomy and connectedness characteristics; and a mean of 21 percent (SD = .20) consisted of autonomy characteristics.

Although most of the participants described themselves in autonomous terms, it is interesting to note that in a European American sample not all did. Moreover, autonomy characteristics were less prevalent than connectedness characteristics, as well as interrelated autonomy and connectedness characteristics, both in terms of the proportion of participants who mentioned them and also in terms of the mean proportion of the participants' self statements. Much has clearly been made of European American autonomy values, but this finding suggests that, as expected, other aspects of the self are at least as important during late adolescence. Indeed, for some time now research has suggested that adolescence for European Americans is not a time that is devoted only to constructing a separate self but of reorganizing previous social ties and constructing oneself in relation to new social groups (see Harter, 1999; Newman, 1989; Steinberg and Silverberg, 1986; Youniss and Smollar, 1985). In addition, this sample consisted solely of late adolescents who are attending college. College is certainly a context of individual academic pursuit, but it is also an intensely social context that offers varied opportunities for undergraduates to focus on constructing themselves in relation to others.

Analyses of variance (ANOVA) were conducted, indicating that there were no differences in these overall means according to the participants' socioeconomic backgrounds. It has been suggested that people of lower socioeconomic status tend to be relatively interdependence-oriented, in contrast to people of higher socioeconomic status (Triandis, 1995). On the other hand, some research suggests that children from low socioeconomic households have more experience with some modes of autonomy than children in higher socioeconomic households because they may leave school early to work, which enables them to become self-reliant earlier (Fasick, 1984). Other research with European American parents of varied educational backgrounds indicates that they all place relatively equal value on fostering their children's autonomy and connectedness (Raeff, 2000). Although the current findings corroborate the position that autonomy and connectedness co-occur and are equally prevalent aspects of the self for varied groups of people, it is also possible that the common college experience erased any socioeconomic differences that might have existed between the two groups. Further research is required to investigate how autonomy and connectedness are evident among late adolescents with more clearly differentiated socioeconomic experiences.

There were differences by gender, with males more likely than females to discuss autonomy characteristics ($F = 6.56$, $p < .015$) and females more likely than males to discuss interrelated autonomy and connectedness characteristics ($F = 6.54$, $p < .015$). In one way, these findings are in keeping with the position that males are more likely than females to focus on autonomy (Gilligan, 1982). In another way, however, these findings do not tell a clear-cut story about gender and the self. That is, there were no gender differences in connectedness self-characteristics, only in autonomy self-characteristics and interrelated autonomy and connectedness self-characteristics. Thus connectedness characteristics may be just as much a part of the self for males as for females. Similarly, autonomy characteristics may be just as much a part of the self for females as for males. In this study, the difference between males and females lies in the greater likelihood for females to conceptualize their autonomy characteristics in conjunction with connectedness characteristics. We will return to trying to understand gender differences when the autonomy self-characteristics are presented later.

Also, as expected, the participants' self-conceptions consisted of multifaceted connectedness and autonomy characteristics, as well as varied interrelated autonomy and connectedness characteristics. The coding categories for the most frequent multifaceted autonomy and connectedness dimensions are defined next, and interview quotations are provided to illustrate each coding category. The prevalence of each coding category in the participants' interviews is also given. Qualitative analyses of the most frequent interrelated autonomy and connectedness characteristics are then considered in a separate section. An independent judge coded ten (28 percent) of the interviews, and using Cohen's Kappa coefficient, there was 82 percent reliability for these coding categories.

Multifaceted Connectedness Characteristics of the Self. _GENERAL SOCIABILITY_ consisted of descriptions of oneself in terms of modes of interacting with varied people (interview examples: "I'm very outgoing"; "I'm a people person"). Of the thirty-three participants who discussed connectedness self-characteristics, twenty-nine (88 percent) described themselves in terms of general sociability. In addition, general sociability accounted for a mean of 72 percent (SD = .37) of the participants' connectedness characteristics.

WIDER SOCIAL CONCERNS involved descriptions of oneself in terms of wider societal issues, societal standards, social roles, or group membership (interview examples: "I follow the rules"; "I was on student council"). Of the thirty-three participants who discussed connectedness self-characteristics, ten (30 percent) described themselves in terms of wider social concerns. In addition, wider social concerns accounted for a mean of 17 percent (SD = .30) of the participants' connectedness characteristics.

SOCIAL ACTIVITIES involved self-descriptions in terms of activities carried out with others (interview example: "I play baseball"). Of the thirty-three participants who discussed connectedness self-characteristics, five (15 percent) described themselves in terms of social activities. In addition, social activities accounted for a mean of 5 percent (SD = .14) of the participants' connectedness characteristics.

SPECIFIC RELATIONSHIPS involved descriptions of oneself in terms of direct relationships (interview examples: "I have friends and acquaintances"; "I'm pretty much my father's son"). Of the thirty-three participants who discussed connectedness self-characteristics, four (12 percent) described themselves in terms of specific relationships. In addition, specific relationships accounted for a mean of 4 percent (SD = .12) of the participants' connectedness characteristics.

The results for these multifaceted connectedness self-characteristics clearly point to the prevalence of being generally sociable. The high proportion of general sociability reflects the openness, and even fluidity, of American relationships. This finding also reflects the historically derived American cultural value that people are ideally free and equal (Raeff, 1997a, 1997b). Accordingly, structuring relationships among free and equal individuals involves being able to enter into and negotiate relationships with varied social partners. This view of the self in relation to others may be contrasted with research that shows how some social self-characteristics among non-Westerners consist of concrete, role-related activities, or automatic social obligations within specific, hierarchically structured relationships (Greenfield and Suzuki, 1998; Shweder and Bourne, 1984). Although specific relationships and contributing to society may be important within the American cultural context, the focus remains on being able to establish and maintain relationships with anyone whom one might encounter during varied daily life situations (see also Raeff, 2000). Moreover, general sociability gives the individual a stance that embraces all people equally, and people within specific relationships or in-groups (for example, family members) are not singled out for differential treatment.

Multifaceted Autonomy Characteristics of the Self. MENTALLY SEPARATE involved describing oneself as a mentally or cognitively separate person, interview examples: "I'm intelligent"; "I'm opinionated"), of the twenty-four participants who discussed autonomy self-characteristics nine (38 percent) described themselves in terms of being mentally separate. In addition, being mentally separate accounted for a mean of 15 percent (SD = .21) of the participants' autonomy characteristics.

PHYSICALLY SEPARATE consisted of describing oneself as a physically separate person (interview examples: "I'm athletic"; "I'm in good health"). Of the twenty-four participants who discussed autonomy self-characteristics, nine (38 percent) described themselves in terms of being physically separate. In addition, being physically separate accounted for a mean of 20 percent (SD = .31) of the participants' autonomy characteristics.

SELF-MOTIVATION involved describing oneself as the source of one's own actions (interview examples: "I'm determined"; "I make my own decisions"). Of the twenty-four participants who discussed autonomy self-characteristics, nine (38 percent) described themselves in terms of self-motivation. In addition, self-motivation accounted for a mean of 23 percent (SD = .35) of the participants' autonomy characteristics.

SEPARATE ACTIVITIES involved defining oneself in terms of activities conducted alone, or in terms of finding fulfillment through activities conducted alone (interview examples: "I'd rather stay home and study"; "I like to read"). Of the twenty-four participants who discussed autonomy self-characteristics, eight (33 percent) described themselves in terms of separate activities. In addition, separate activities accounted for a mean of 17 percent (SD = .30) of the participants' autonomy characteristics.

SELF-RELIANCE involved describing oneself as a person who can handle varied life tasks on one's own (interview examples: "I can handle a lot of stuff"; "I don't have to depend on anyone else to get along"). Of the twenty-four participants who discussed autonomy self-characteristics, four (17 percent) described themselves in terms of being self-reliant. In addition, being self-reliant accounted for a mean of 10 percent ($SD = .29$) of the participants' autonomy characteristics.

SELF-INSULATION consisted of describing oneself as a person who protects himself or herself from stress or problems (interview examples: "I'm easygoing"; "I don't let many things get to me"). Of the twenty-four participants who discussed autonomy self-characteristics, three (13 percent) described themselves in terms of self-insulation. In addition, self-insulation accounted for a mean of 6 percent ($SD = .21$) of the participants' autonomy characteristics.

SELF-CONFIDENCE involved defining oneself as a person who is confident in his or her own abilities (interview example: "I've just got uh, high self-confidence, I guess. I'm sure of myself. I don't second-guess myself a lot"). Of the twenty-four participants who discussed autonomy self-characteristics, one (4 percent) described the self in terms of confidence, and it accounted for a mean of 1 percent ($SD = .07$) of the participants' autonomy characteristics.

SELF-FULFILLMENT involved descriptions of oneself in terms of being fulfilled as a separate person (interview example: "What I do is what makes me happy so I'm not going to do something else to make [others] happy"). Of the twenty-four participants who discussed autonomy self-characteristics, one (4 percent) described the self in terms of self-fulfillment; self-fulfillment accounted for a mean of 1 percent ($SD = .07$) of the participants' autonomy characteristics.

Overall, these multifaceted autonomy self-characteristics reflect American values that humans are separate beings with their own ideas and preferences who ideally pursue self-chosen goals. An ANOVA indicates that there were gender differences for the physically separate autonomy self-characteristic, with males more likely than females to describe themselves as physically separate ($F = 5.94$, $p < .023$). Indeed, no females described themselves as physically separate, whereas being physically separate accounted for a mean of 30 percent ($SD = .34$) of the males' autonomy self-characteristics. In addition, for most of the males using this category involved describing oneself as athletic. This finding, in conjunction with the overall gender differences presented earlier, suggests that males may not be more likely than females to see themselves as psychologically autonomous, just as more athletic. In addition, this finding is in keeping with research demonstrating that females, from late childhood through adolescence, are significantly more likely than males to report unfavorable self-perceptions of their athletic competencies (Harter, 1999). Thus, when describing themselves females may simply opt not to mention this perceived negative self-characteristic.

This set of autonomy self-characteristics is notable for the very low frequency of some characteristics that, from a dichotomous perspective on autonomy and connectedness, would be deemed important for European

American self-development, namely, self-confidence and self-fulfillment. Self-confidence and self-fulfillment represent specific instances of achieving a sense of worth, esteem, or general well-being on one's own, and it has been suggested that achieving such positive self-feelings as a separate individual is more likely in so-called independence-oriented cultures than in so-called interdependence cultures (Markus and Kitayama, 1991; Triandis, 1995). However, there is much research on the development of self-esteem that points to how children and adolescents evaluate themselves in relation to varied other people (Harter, 1999).

Moreover, the current findings regarding the low proportions of self-confidence and self-fulfillment point to the importance of not adhering too strictly to preconceived notions about autonomy and connectedness, without investigating people's subjective experiences of the self as autonomous and connected within a particular culture. That is, rather than defining autonomy in terms of a set of specific characteristics (such as self-confidence, self-fulfillment, self-reliance), it may make more sense to begin with a general and universally applicable definition of autonomy, and then through empirical research one could discern the varied cultural manifestations of that general definition. For example, autonomy may generally be defined as those aspects of a person's functioning and experience that involve being mentally and physically separate. The current study sheds some light on how this general definition is specifically manifest among European Americans in terms of viewing oneself as a mentally and physically separate being who is the source of his or her own choices and behavior. Cross-cultural research is required to discern other specific manifestations of autonomy in varied cultural contexts.

When considering these multifaceted autonomy self-characteristics in conjunction with the multifaceted connectedness self-characteristics already presented here, it is evident that they are compatible, and that they do not preclude one another. For example, it is possible to be generally sociable and also self-motivated. Thus, being connected to others and being autonomous are both valued self-characteristics that can serve different functions. However, just because conflicts between connectedness and autonomy self-characteristics were not apparent in the participants' discussions, it does not mean that conflicts never occur. Indeed, I suspect that total harmony between varied autonomy and connectedness characteristics would be too good to be true. Thus, further research is required, perhaps involving more pointed questions about conflicting self-dimensions. Nevertheless, the current data do indicate that conflict is not inherent to the co-occurrence of connectedness and autonomy self-characteristics.

Interrelated Autonomy and Connectedness Self-Characteristics. In presenting the multifaceted interrelated autonomy and connectedness characteristics that emerged in the interviews, it is important to point out that identifying these characteristics involves a key methodological issue that also has implications for moving beyond a dichotomous approach to autonomy

and connectedness. In particular, the study points to the importance of probing participants' initial self-descriptions in order to discern whether they represent issues of autonomy, connectedness, or both. An investigator may have
some preconceived notions of certain autonomy and connectedness characteristics, but those notions may or may not be compatible with a participant's
subjective understanding of himself or herself. Moreover, a participant's subjective understanding of a stated self-characteristic may not be immediately
obvious, thus requiring some further probing. To illustrate this problem
more concretely, let us consider some specific interview cases.

In response to the general self-conceptualization question ("How
would you describe yourself; tell me about yourself; who are you?"), one
female participant responded, "I would say um, insightful." At first glance,
and from a dichotomous approach to autonomy and connectedness, it is
easy to interpret this statement in terms of autonomy. That is, this person
is describing herself as a separate mental being in terms of a generally positively valued cognitive ability. However, when the interviewer asked her
why being insightful is important, this participant replied: "Well, for me it's
very important because communication's obviously an important thing for
everything and every facet of life. But I just, it makes me feel good to have
that insight because. . . . I don't know. . . . I feel like I'm helping them in a
way by trying to understand them. . . . It makes me feel like I've put forth
an effort and. . . . I don't know."

To further understand this statement, the interviewer then asked, "An
effort to do [what]?", and the participant responded: "An effort to understand where someone's coming from. And some people. . . . You know like
most people I would say, kind of with their busy lives, kind of just, you
know [say], uh, this is what I need, this is what I want. You know, and sometimes it's nice to have insight into what somebody else is thinking and feeling. So it just makes life kind of run a little smoother." This excerpt shows
that asking the participant why being insightful is an important self-
characteristic pointed to its inseparability from issues of general sociability
and the subsequent probe further elucidated the social implications of her
separate cognitive ability.

Another interview excerpt offers an example of how asking about the
importance of a self-characteristic is required to understand that viewing
oneself as mentally separate may be inseparable from viewing oneself in
relation to wider social concerns. This time, a male participant described
himself as "very intellectually focused." When asked to explain the importance of this characteristic, the participant responded: "Well, I want to be a
Supreme Court justice. So you have to have an educational background."
When asked why he wants to be a Supreme Court justice, he replied: "It's,
well, the most, you know, the highest position you can get in the legal pro-
fession, the legal field. It's the way to have the most impact on a wide scale."

Thus far, these examples point to how an initially stated autonomy self-
characteristic is related to social issues. In addition, the interviews show

how initially stated social self-characteristics may be related to autonomy self-characteristics. This kind of interrelation may actually be apparent even before probing when a participant claims to like or enjoy some social self-characteristic, thereby suggesting that social characteristics are a source of individual fulfillment. For example, when asked to describe herself one participant said: "I like to help people a lot. I like to get their spirits going and make them think high [sic] of themself [sic]." Saying that she likes to help others already implies that helping others is a source of self-fulfillment. Asking her about the importance of helping others further elucidated how this social self-characteristic is a source of individual self-fulfillment. The participant explained that being helpful is important "because it makes me feel good about myself. And it makes me feel like I did a good deed, so I can be happy for the day." In this way, we see how the general sociability self-characteristic has implications for individual self-fulfillment.

A variation on this theme that fulfillment can be achieved socially was evident among study participants who discussed how they feel supported or comforted through social ties. For example, one participant said that being outgoing is important because it enables him to make friends. Friends, in turn, are important "just because I think the more friends you have around you, the more people you have to fall back on if something troublesome comes up in your life. Like um, everybody goes through tough times financially, you know, mentally, physically." For another participant, having close relationships is important "just to, you know, help you through rough times. You know, just enjoy the good ones."

These kinds of examples that illustrate the importance of going beyond asking participants to generate a list of self-characteristics were also found among the majority of interrelated autonomy and connectedness self-characteristics. That is, of the thirty-four participants who discussed interrelated autonomy and connectedness self-characteristics, twenty-seven (79 percent) described themselves in terms of being fulfilled or supported through connectedness characteristics, including general sociability, specific relationships, and social activities. This finding helps to refute the argument, stemming from a dichotomous approach to autonomy and connectedness, that Americans are typically focused on finding self-fulfillment through their own individual achievements, and not in terms of relationships with others. Similarly, finding fulfillment through connectedness points to how relationships are viewed as enriching, not shackling, aspects of life, leaving people neither isolated nor lonely. This finding also helps to explain the notable lack of self-fulfillment in the autonomy self-characteristics.

In addition, of the thirty-four participants who discussed interrelated autonomy and connectedness self-characteristics, eleven (32 percent) discussed how their separate cognitive abilities affect their general sociability or their wider social concerns. In keeping with the expectation that autonomy and connectedness self-characteristics would be interrelated in multifaceted ways, some other interrelated autonomy and connectedness characteristics also emerged but occurred less frequently than the interrelated characteristics just mentioned. For example, of the thirty-four participants who discussed interrelated autonomy and connectedness self-characteristics, three (9 percent) mentioned how they could improve themselves by being generally sociable. One of these three participants described himself as outgoing, and this general sociability characteristic is important to him because it enables him to meet people and make more friends. Having friends is in turn important because "it's good to have a different influence on your life other than just your family because those kids are influenced by their families. So you're influenced by different views from them indirectly."

One participant discussed how being fulfilled as a separate person makes sociability easier. He said, "I like to be happy, make people laugh if I can. . . . If you're like moping around, you're gonna bring other people down. You're not gonna be the kind of person they're gonna want to hang out with." This same participant also discussed how being confident is inseparable from general sociability. He said, "If you have a poor self image. . . . you won't go out, you won't talk to people."

Overall, these qualitative analyses of interrelated autonomy and connectedness self-characteristics point to how the participants are defining themselves as individuals in relation to others. Moreover, these findings indicate that autonomy and connectedness are not simply coexisting aspects of the self. Instead, dimensions of autonomy and connectedness may be interrelated in complex ways, indicating how they are inseparable, and mutually constitutive aspects of the self.

Becoming Oneself. The participants' reflections regarding how they got to be the way they are today were coded in terms of whether they identified social issues and/or their own individual contributions. For this question, there was 100 percent interrater reliability with an independent judge who coded seven (20 percent) of the interviews.

Eighty-six percent of the participants claimed to be the way they are because of their social experiences and interpersonal relationships, especially with family, friends, or teachers. For example, one participant said, "I guess through, actually through my dad. . . . I guess like. . . . I guess the way I grew up and my father. . . . I don't know, like the school that I attended and stuff. . . . The friends that I had."

Another participant said, "Uh a combination of things like, you know, the influence of my parents. . . . And then like the people I hung around with when I was younger also like shaped my values and everything. . . . My older brother, he probably had like the biggest influence on me, you know. Uh, like he'd start up something, and then I'd start doing that. . . . So, like I got a lot of, uh, I guess my values and stuff from him. And also from school. And uh like teachers influenced me. And uh, people I went to school with."

The remaining 14 percent attributed the way they are today to a combination of social experiences and individual effort. For example, one participant said, "Basic training helped a lot. My mom. My dad was always gone, so it was my mom pretty much. And just, and just myself. Just looking at what I want to do, doing what I want to do."

These results stand somewhat in contrast to the interpretation of the *New York Times Magazine* survey discussed earlier. The difference may be attributed, in part, to methodology. That is, the current study leaves more room for a participant's subjective reflections on the issue of how he or she became who he or she is, in contrast to the survey's imposition of certain categories. The current study specifically included college undergraduates, whereas the *New York Times Magazine* survey more generally targeted people over eighteen and therefore probably included more adults than late adolescents. Accordingly, the results may also be understood through differences in sampling characteristics. Nevertheless, the current findings support the view that European Americans do not view themselves exclusively as self-made individuals whose development is unaffected by social factors.

Conclusions

The results of this study provide support for the theoretical position that autonomy and connectedness represent multifaceted and interrelated aspects of the self, which in turn reflect cultural values about independent and social functioning. In addition, these data indicate the importance of connectedness, as well as autonomy, in a sample of late adolescent European Americans. Not only are European Americans in general stereotypically characterized in terms of autonomy, but adolescents in particular are often assumed to be focusing mainly on issues of separation and individuation. However, the current data suggest that late adolescents are reorganizing themselves in relation to others, since they are certainly not becoming independent without being simultaneously connected to others. Further research with children and younger adolescents is required to identify developmental trajectories for how autonomy and connectedness become increasingly differentiated and integrated aspects of the self in varied cultural contexts.

The current study also has implications for conceptualizing the self and culture more generally. In particular, the results of this study point to the utility of conceptualizing both the self and culture as systems (von Bertalanffy, 1968, 1969). According to von Bertalanffy, a system is "a complex of interacting elements" (1968, p. 42), or a "set of elements standing in interrelations" (1969, p. 55). Thus, as a system the self consists of varied dynamically interrelated parts, including the dimensions of autonomy and connectedness identified in this chapter. As a system, culture consists of varied interrelated patterns of behavior that reflect varied interrelated values, including values about independent and social functioning. Conceptualizing the self and culture as systems points to the importance of further investigating not only how their respective parts are interrelated but also how selves and cultures affect each other's systemic functioning as they engage in ongoing dynamic interactions. Ultimately, furthering our understanding of the dynamic and complex interrelations that exist among varied self and cultural systems around the world may also further our understanding of human functioning in our global world system.

References

von Bertalanffy, L.. *Organismic Psychology and Systems Theory*. Barre, Mass.: Clark University Press, with Barre Publishers, 1968.

von Bertalanffy, L.. *General System Theory*. New York: Braziller, 1969.

Damon, W., and Hart, D. *Self-Understanding in Childhood and Adolescence*. Cambridge: Cambridge University Press, 1988.

Erikson, E. H. *Identity and the Life Cycle*. New York: Norton, 1980. (Originally published 1959)

Fasick, F. A. "Parents, Peers, Youth Culture and Autonomy in Adolescence." *Adolescence*, 1984, *19*, 143–157.

Gilligan, C. *In a Different Voice: Psychological Theory and Women's Development*. Cambridge, Mass.: Harvard University Press, 1982.

Greenfield, P. M., and Suzuki, L. K. "Culture and Human Development: Implications for Parenting, Education, Pediatrics, and Mental Health." In I. E. Sigel and K. A. Renninger (eds.), *Handbook of Child Psychology: Vol. 4*. New York: Wiley, 1998.

Grotevant, H. D., and Cooper, C. R. "Individuality and Connectedness in Adolescent Development: Review and Prospects for Research on Identity, Relationships, and Context." In E.E.A. Skoe and A.L.v.d. Lippe (eds.), *Personality Development in Adolescence*. London: Routledge, 1998.

Guisinger, S., and Blatt, S. J. "Individuality and Relatedness: Evolution of a Fundamental Dialectic." *American Psychologist*, 1994, *49*, 104–111.

Harter, S. *The Construction of the Self*. New York: Guilford Press, 1999.

James, W. *The Principles of Psychology*. Cambridge, Mass.: Harvard University Press, 1983. (Originally published 1890)

Josselson, R. "Identity and Relatedness in the Life Cycle." In H. A. Bosma, T. G. Graafsma, H. D. Grotevant, and D. J. de Levita (eds.), *Identity and Development*. Thousand Oaks, Calif.: Sage, 1994.

Marková, I. "The Individual and Society in Psychological Theory." *Theory and Psychology*, 2000, *10*, 107–116.

Markus, H. R., and Kitayama, S. "Culture and the Self: Implications for Cognition, Emotion, and Motivation." *Psychological Review*, 1991, *98*, 224–253.

Markus, H. R., and Kitayama, S. "A Collective Fear of the Collective: Implications for Selves and Theories of Selves." *Personality and Social Psychology Bulletin*, 1994, *20*, 568–579.

Mead, G. H. *Mind, Self, and Society*. Chicago: University of Chicago Press, 1962. (Originally published 1934)

Mines, M. "Conceptualizing the Person: Hierarchical Society and Individual Autonomy in India." *American Anthropologist*, 1988, *90*, 568–579.

Newman, B. M. "The Changing Nature of the Parent-Adolescent Relationship from Early to Late Adolescence." *Adolescence*, 1989, i24, 915–924.

Odin, S. *The Social Self in Zen and American Pragmatism*. Albany: State University of New York Press, 1996.

Offer, D., Ostrov, E., Howard, K. I, and Atkinson, R. *The Teenage World: Adolescents' Self-Image in Ten Countries*. New York: Plenum Medical, 1988.

Oyserman, D., Coon, H. M., and Kemmelmeier, M. "Rethinking Individualism and Collectivism: Evaluation of Theoretical Assumptions and Meta-Analyses." *Psychological Bulletin*, 2002, *128*, 3–72.

Piaget, J. *The Origin of Intelligence in the Child.* London: Routledge and Kegan Paul, 1953.

Raeff, C. "Individuals in Relationships: Cultural Values, Children's Social Interactions, and the Development of an American Individualistic Self." *Developmental Review,* 1997a, *17,* 205–238.

Raeff, C. "Maintaining Cultural Coherence in the Midst of Cultural Diversity." *Developmental Review,* 1997b, *17,* 250–261.

Raeff, C. "European-American Parents' Ideas About Their Toddlers' Independence and Interdependence." *Journal of Applied Developmental Psychology,* 2000 *21,* 183–205.

Raeff, C. *Always Separate, Always Connected: Some Interrelations Between Independence and Interdependence in Cultural Contexts of Development.* Mahwah, N.J.: Erlbaum, forthcoming.

Rosenberger, N. R. (ed.), *Japanese Sense of Self.* Cambridge: Cambridge University Press, 1992.

Sampson, E. E. "Psychology and the American Ideal." *Journal of Personality and Social Psychology,* 1977, *35,* 767–782.

Sampson, E. E. "The Challenge of Social Change for Psychology: Globalization and Psychology's Theory of the Person." *American Psychologist,* 1989, *44,* 914–921.

Sampson, E. E. "Reinterpreting Individualism and Collectivism." *American Psychologist,* 2000, *55,* 1425–1432.

Shweder, R. A., and Bourne, E. J. "Does the Concept of the Person Vary Cross-Culturally?" In R. A. Shweder and R. A. LeVine (eds.), *Culture Theory.* Cambridge: Cambridge University Press, 1984.

Spiro, M. E. "Is the Western Conception of the Self Peculiar Within the Context of the World Cultures?" *Ethos,* 1993, *21,* 107–153.

Steinberg, L., and Silverberg, S. B. "The Vicissitudes of Autonomy in Early Adolescence." *Child Development,* 1986, *57,* 841–851.

Triandis, H. C. *Individualism and Collectivism.* Boulder, Colo.: Westview Press, 1995.

Turiel, E. "Equality and Hierarchy: Conflict in Values." In E. S. Reed, E. Turiel, and T. Brown (eds.), *Values and Knowledge.* Mahwah, N.J.: Erlbaum, 1996.

Užgiris, I. "Infants in Relation: Performers, Pupils, and Partners." In W. Damon (ed.), *Child Development Today and Tomorrow.* San Francisco: Jossey-Bass, 1989.

Waterman, A. S. "Identity as an Aspect of Optimal Psychological Functioning." In G. R. Adams, T. P. Gullota, and R. Montemayor (eds.), *Advances in Adolescent Development,* Vol. 4. Thousand Oaks, Calif.: Sage, 1992.

Youniss, J., and Smollar, J. *Adolescent Relations with Mothers, Fathers, and Friends.* Chicago: University of Chicago Press, 1985.

Catherine Raeff is associate professor of psychology at Indiana University of Pennsylvania, Indiana, Pennsylvania.

5

Selves and cultures are not independent entities. Focusing on the processes by which individuals and cultures participate in each other's functioning, we can begin to understand how personal and communal dimensions of selfhood must be represented in some form in all the world's cultures.

The Coactive Construction of Selves in Cultures

Michael F. Mascolo

The contributors to this volume have reviewed research that builds upon, and yet challenges, presuppositions of the individualism-collectivist (I-C) framework as it relates to the development of self. Each contributor has argued some variation on the theme that both individual and communal dimensions of self are necessarily represented in all cultural groups in some form. As such, to represent the full complexity of cultural meaning, it becomes important to identify unique ways in which individual and communal dimensions of selfhood are represented in relation to each other within members of a given cultural group.

The idea that the twin issues of individuality and collectivity must be represented in some way in all cultures raises questions about the very concept of culture and its relation to developing selves. Researchers in the I-C tradition have amassed compelling evidence demonstrating meaningful differences in how members from different societies construct representations of self. However, although such studies have identified meaningful *differences* in the world's cultures, it is important to discriminate the *use* of culture as a variable in cross-cultural research from the *concept* of culture in developmental theory. When we perform cross-cultural research, we use culture as a methodological tool. This practice provides an indispensable methodological tool, but it is important that theorists avoid reducing the concept of *culture* to an external variable.

In everyday interaction, individuals and cultures do not operate as separable entities. Any psychological act necessarily occurs within the medium of culture (Cole, 1996). In so doing, people and cultures function as actual *parts* of each other's processes (Shweder, 1991). What conceptions of self and culture can accommodate this view? How can we perform research that illuminates the ways in which selves and cultures "make each other up" (Shweder and Sullivan, 1993)? To answer these questions, there is a need to develop a model of the processes by which selves and cultures participate in each other's functioning over time. To develop such a model, the discussion turns to analysis of three issues that undergird research related to the development of selves within cultures: (1) To what do we refer when we speak of *self*? (2) What do we mean by *culture*? (3) How can we understand the relations between selves and cultures?

The Concept of Self

To what do the terms *I, me,* and *mine* refer? At its most basic, when asked to identify the self an individual might simply point to his or her body. However, people use the term *self* and its cognates to refer to different aspects of an individual and his or her psychological processes. One might suggest three categories of self-relevant experience: (1) conscious, self-directed action on objects; (2) reflexive self-consciousness; and (3) higher-order theories of self.

Primary Conscious Activity. The most basic level of selfhood consists of the capacity for self-directed conscious action on physical and social objects. Primary conscious action consists of *directed awareness in action*. Such activity exhibits several important properties. First, conscious activity involves a degree of self-regulation in the sense that the actor exerts some control over his or her action. Second, conscious activity is *intentional* in the sense that it is always directed toward some object; it is *about* something (Searle, 1983). Third, conscious activity is *constructive* in the sense that it plays an active role in constructing its own objects (Merleau-Ponty, 1945). As a result, the objects of consciousness need not be tangible; they include imaginings and impossible objects. Fourth, conscious action is *integrative*. With the exception of pathological circumstances, any psychological act necessarily involves some integration of psychological systems (that is, motive-relevant appraisals of the world, affective experience, muscle action; Lewis, 1990; Mascolo and Harkins, 1998). Primary conscious activity is represented at point A1 in Figure 5.1.

Self-directed conscious activity constitutes the most basic form of integrated action. For example, two-month-olds are able to pull a string in order to bring about an interesting audiovisual display. When the arm-pull-display contingency is terminated, the infants accelerate their arm pulling and evince angry facial actions (Lewis, Alessandri, and Sullivan, 1990). Such infants are engaging in a primitive form of goal-directed action (arm pulling). The conscious object of their activity is the sensorimotor experience of their arm pull and audiovisual display. Thus, in primary conscious action, individuals exhibit consciousness *of* action and outcomes, but they are not explicitly conscious "*that* I am acting."

Figure 5.1. Coactions Among Individual-Culture Systems

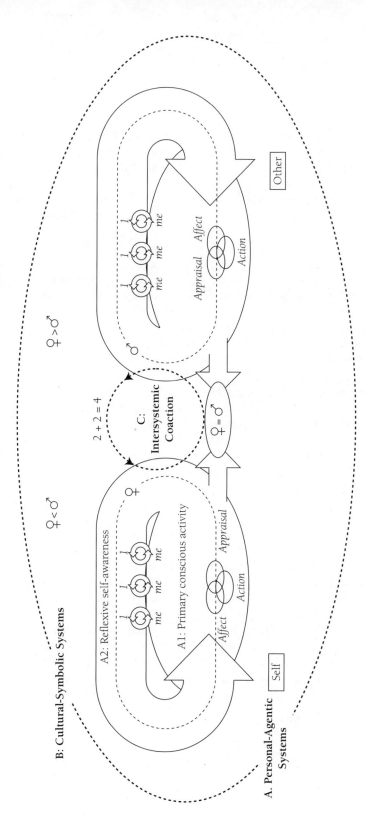

Selves develop through intersystemic coaction among personal, social, and cultural systems (point C). Primary conscious activity (A1) is composed of coactions between motive-relevant appraisals, affect, and action on physical and social objects in the world. In social interaction, partners coregulate each other's activity as they adjust their thinking, feeling, and acting to each other over time (C). In coregulated exchanges, selves are born as an individual's consciousness is directed upon itself (A2). Reflective self-awareness involves temporally organized I-me exchanges as indicated by James, Mead, and others. Selves become transformed over time as individuals use sign-mediated cultural meanings (B) to represent and regulate self in relation to others.

Self-Conscious Action. The sense of self is born when an individual becomes capable of turning primary conscious activity upon itself. In so doing, one becomes capable of self-conscious action. This is represented in Figure 5.1 in terms of the self-reflexive arrow at point A2. The capacity for self-conscious activity develops gradually, taking different forms over the first two years of life (Mascolo and Fischer, 1998). Early self-conscious emotions (pride, embarrassment) begin to emerge in American and Western European children in the second year.

As elaborated by Mead (1932) and others (Cooley, 1902; Damon and Hart, 1988; James, 1890; Harter, 1999), self-conscious experience consists of an *I* phase and a *me* phase. The sense of *I* reflects the sense of personal agency—the elusive awareness that it is *I* who exerts control over a particular action or component of action. The sense of *me* consists of the experience of self as an object of awareness (see also Lewis and Brooks-Gunn, 1978). This can take many forms, including awareness of parts of the body or of one's own goals, desires, feelings, evaluations, action, and so on, as well as one's sense of social identity (for instance, "Who am I in relation to others?"). As suggested by James (1890) and echoed by others (Gergen, 1992; Hermans and Kempen, 1993; Shotter, 1997), with development people construct many social identities in relation to different interlocutors and social partners.

Higher-Order Self-Representations. As elaborated by Mead, the experience of *I* and *me* is not simply of different *aspects* of self; instead, they consist of different *phases* of self-experience. As consciousness takes itself as an object, the experienced *I* of one moment becomes the experienced *me* of the next. Over time, I-me exchanges are coordinated into higher-order representations. These representations take multiple forms. To the extent that the self consists of a type of *awareness*, it follows that any meaningful sense of selfhood must take into consideration consistency or continuity over time. This necessarily requires the capacity to recollect and organize representations of self into a temporal and narrative form (Bruner and Kalmar, 1998; de Rivera and Sarbin, 1998; Kihlstrom, Beer, and Klein, 2002; McAdams, 1993). As such, the acquisition of a self-narrative constitutes a nontrivial aspect of selfhood. However, higher-order selves are not simply temporal representations. People also construct *theories* of self that are abstracted across time (Harre, 1983; Moshman, 1999). Such self-theories take many forms, including complex ideologies, models, or systems of belief about one's position in a sociomoral order (Harre, 1983), representations of relations among multiple identities, models of the nature of one's psyche or personhood, and ideologies about the nature of self in society.

Culture as a Distributive Process

Like the notion of self, the concept of *culture* is a troublesome one. There are at least three categories of culture theories. For some scholars, culture refers to something that exists outside of the individual—in the environment in some way. For example, Bond and Smith (1996) write: "We adopt Poortinga's (1992) broad position on culture as a set of 'shared constraints that limit the behavior repertoire available to members of a certain. . . . group' (p. 10). This definition of culture may be married to a position of universals, in which 'it is assumed that the same psychological processes are operating in all humans independent of culture' (Poortinga, 1992, p. 13). Cultural constraints then limit and shape the behavioral expression of the universal process" (p. 209).

In defining the goals of psychological science as articulating the nature of cultural universals, this conception clearly defines culture as a variable that functions externally to individuals. The study of culture is less important than articulation of the psychological universals that they limit.

A second group of scholars, most notably cognitive anthropologists (D'Angrade, 1995; Strauss and Quinn, 1997; Spiro, 1987), proceed from the assumption that culture and environment are unintelligible unless their meanings are represented by construing individuals. As such, these scholars are interested in identifying the shared meaning systems that exist within the psyches of individual persons. For example, Spiro (1987) argued "cultural doctrines, ideas, values and the like exist in the minds of social actors—where else *could* they exist?" (p. 161). From this view, culture is located within people in the form of meanings that guide the parsing of personal and social experience within a given community.

The distinction between "inner" and "outer" models of culture (de Munck, 2000) illustrates an important tension in attempts to define the concept of culture. On the one hand, culture is broadly recognized as a process that exists prior to and beyond particular individuals; culture is a public something. One the other hand, public symbols cannot be understood independently of the personal meaning systems of individuals. How can one resolve this antinomy?

One solution is to think of culture as a dynamic distribution of meanings. From this view, one might define culture as a dynamic distribution of systems of meanings, practices, and artifacts throughout a linguistic community. Cultural-symbolic systems are represented in Figure 5.1 at point B in the guise of symbolic forms (especially sign activity) that function both within and beyond the dyad. Thinking of culture in terms of the distribution of meanings helps to address a series of problems. First, if cultural meanings are distributed, the problem of the location of meanings ceases to exist. Meanings are properties of the activities that occur within and between persons and are not fixed forms that exist either in the head or in the environment. Culture exists in the contours of a computer keyboard, in the personal meanings that a person draws upon to use the keyboard, and the Websites distributed throughout the Internet.

Second, to think of culture in terms of distributed systems of meanings and practices underscores the multiplicity of meanings that compose a culture. The commonly held view of culture as a set of shared meanings suggests a common core of meanings that are nested within all members of a community. However, it is unlikely that this idealization ever occurs. In a society, there are enclaves of meaning and practice with which a given individual has little direct contact (for example, practices that exist within industry, an inner city, the national government). These meaning systems can be regarded as parts of culture even if they are not shared by the broader community of which they are a part. Further, the idea that cultures are composed of shared meaning systems obscures the conflicts about meaning and practice that exist within cultures (Abu-Lughod, 1991). To think of cultures as systems of distributed meanings allows and even embraces the idea that cultures can be defined by their internal conflicts.

Third, the idea that cultures are dynamic implies that they are not fixed entities. The elements of culture—its members, practices, technologies, and artifacts—change over time. Even cultures that remain stable over decades or centuries exhibit elements of dynamism; stability requires the expenditure of energy to maintain equilibrium in response to threats that arise both within and outside a culture.

The Construction of Self at the Nexus of Intersystemic Activity

Having offered a conception of the twin processes of *self* and *culture*, one can examine the dynamic interplay between them. One might suggest that selves emerge and undergo developmental transformation at the nexus of intersystemic activity. Selves emerge through *coactions* among multileveled individual-culture systems; no single process or system is primary in the construction of selves (Gottlieb, 1997; Mascolo, Fischer, and Li, 2003). The systems that make up individual-culture relations *coregulate* each other in the development of selves. In making this statement, we avoid reducing self and its development to any single psychological, social, or cultural processes. The process of intersystemic coaction is represented in Figure 5.1 at point C.

The concept of coregulation is an important one. It stipulates that although elements in a system may be *distinct* from each other as entities (self and other; cognition and affect; genes and environment), they are nonetheless *inseparable* as causal processes in each other's functioning. Thus, in face-to face-interactions, self and other function as distinct individuals with their own dispositions; however, in any interaction, they are inseparable as causal processes in each other's behavior. Coregulation occurs as individuals adjust their thoughts, feelings and actions to the ongoing and anticipated actions of their social partners. Coregulation occurs in any face-to-face encounter. For example, when two children pretend to play mother and daughter, the "mother" must continuously adjust her admonishments to the "daughter's" ongoing transgressions; simultaneously, the "child" adjusts her pleas for clemency to the severity of the "mother's" scolding. In this way, the actions of the other are part of the self's actions and experiences and vice versa (Fogel, 1993; Mascolo, Fischer, and Neimeyer, 1999).

To illustrate the coactive construction of selves within culture, I draw upon observations made by Corsaro (1985), who performed an ethnographic analysis of peer culture in the context of a university-affiliated preschool in a U.S. city. In focusing on the evolution of selves within peer culture, it is assumed that the "peer culture" observed within the particular preschool Corsaro studied is embedded in larger systems of cultural beliefs, values, and practices in the United States. The construction of selves in cultural contexts involves a continuous cascade of processes.

First, *in coregulated activity, social partners seize meanings from broader culture to mediate joint action.* Acting together, partners produce novel meanings and experiences at a level they would ordinarily be incapable of sustaining alone. Corsaro (1985) described interactions among three preschool boys as they developed a game called "The Hunters." In the preschool in question, playing with guns was discouraged by preschool staff. As children in the daycare center became cognizant of their teachers' prohibitions, they began to inhibit direct gun play. Motivated by their continued personal desires to engage in pretend shooting and gun play, the boys gradually modified and transformed existing role-playing games (involving animal and family themes) into a new game. In playing the hunters, the boys would transform their broomsticks—usually used as pretend horses and animals—into guns that they would use to hunt and shoot animals. The transformation of animal play into hunting allowed the boys to engage in gun play in more legitimate ways. As in the game "Cowboys and Indians," the boys use guns to shoot; however, in "The Hunters" the boys shot at animals (to secure food), not at each other. Further, in assigning a dual function to their broomsticks (as horses and as guns), the boys could shift from animal play to gun play in a reasonably discreet manner, thus concealing their gun play from their teachers. In this way, the preschoolers' construction of "The Hunters" illustrates how individuals jointly seize, use, and transform existing cultural rules, meanings, and practices to advance their own agendas.

Second, *sign-mediated interaction often functions to direct attention to one's own actions, thoughts, and feelings.* Selves develop as individuals appropriate jointly constructed meanings to represent and regulate their own actions and experiences. Corsaro (1985) gives several examples of how self-experience is constructed as preschool peers appropriate and transform cultural meanings and resources. One important social concern evinced by the preschoolers was *physical size,* represented as being "big" or "bigger" than others. Children's concern with being big likely arises from their identification of status with qualities that adults have but children do not (their size, ability to be "the boss," use of "dirty language," and the like). In one observation, Corsaro observed this interaction as children played on some climbing bars:

L and V have climbed up to the fourth level of. . . . the bars. . . . L yells to V who is with D near the base of the bars. When V looks up, L. shouts: "We're bigger than you!"

"Oh no you're not!" retorts V, and she begins to climb onto the bars. . . . D follows V and repeats "Oh, no, you're not!". . . . V and D then climb up on the fifth level, and V says: "We are higher now too!" Now all four children chant in unison: "We are higher than anybody else! We are higher than anybody else. . . . We are bigger than anybody else!" [Corsaro, 1985, p. 186].

Within this coregulated interaction, we see how the children use existing cultural artifacts (the climbing structure) and meanings (bigness brings status) in the interactive construction of comparative identity (being "bigger"). The self-referential utterances in these competitive exchanges are coregulated in interesting ways. Not only do the groups of children respond to each other's assertions, but there is a spontaneously evolving vacillation between individual self-expression (that is, when an individual child taunts "We're bigger than you!") and group cohesion (when the group chants this expression). Thus, in these linguistic exchanges children seize broader cultural meanings and resources to jointly construct shared representations of self in relation to others.

Third, *meanings that have been transformed within local social relations can become redistributed among broader cultural systems.* Selves are not the only elements of individual-culture systems that undergo change. Depending on the scope and nature of the cultural processes, a culture changes as a result of coactions among its members. In this way intersystemic coactions come full circle, as cultural forms that are modified in joint exchanges become redeposited into broader cultural systems. This happens nearly every day as novel technologies are disseminated throughout the global marketplace (for example, computer software). Less dramatic but nonetheless genuine examples of "cultural change" occur at more a local level. Corsaro (1985) described how a game called "The Garbage Man" evolved among nursery school children but was maintained long after the children had left the school. On mornings when a garbage truck came to remove refuse from an adjoining dumpster, groups of children would peer through the climbing bars and chant "garbage man!" The children would become excited as the garbage truck emptied the dumpster and would imitate the sounds and actions of the truck. When finished, the drivers would honk their horn to chants of "garbage man!" This practice involved different numbers and combinations of children on a given morning, and it was still ongoing with a different cohort of children a year after Corsaro first took notice of the practice. In this way, a practice that evolved in joint activity became part of the local peer culture.

The Dynamics of Selves Within Cultures

Consider the contrast between two quotes, written by two influential thinkers. The first is from Harry Triandis: "Although some students of culture assume that every culture is unique. . . . science deals with generalizations. Thus, the issue is whether or not the emic elements of culture are of interest. When the emic elements are local adaptations of etic elements, they are of great interest" (1994, p. 20).

In this quote, Triandis articulates the basis of his allegiance to the search for cultural similarities and differences along universalizing dimensions. In this view, local cultural meanings are of interest primarily when they reflect variations on broader universals. Now compare Triandis's view to an oft-quoted passage by Clifford Geertz: "The Western conception of the person as a bounded, unique, more or less integrated motivational and cognitive universe, a dynamic center of awareness, emotion, judgment and action, organized into a distinctive whole and set contrastively against other such wholes and against a social and natural background is, however incorrigible it may seem to us, a rather peculiar idea within the context of the world's cultures" (1979, p. 229).

In Geertz's view, local cultural meanings are of central importance. From this view, what Westerners may see as the ubiquitous basis of selfhood is the exception rather than the rule in the history of the world's cultures.

The evidence reviewed in this volume suggests that in the cultural groups examined, individuals represent themselves consistently in terms of both individual and communal dimensions. Further, the results of infancy research performed over the past decades strongly suggest that the sense of self is organized around a *phenomenal core* (primary conscious activity).

This would include a basic sense of agency and violation (Lewis, Alessandri, and Sullivan, 1990; Stern, 1985), sensorimotor action and proprioception (Fischer and Hogan, 1989; Meltzoff, 1993), affect and the varieties of bodily qualia (Emde, 1983; Legerstee, 1999), a sense of being located in space (Harre and Gillett, 1994), as well as the capacity to construct intersubjective experiences with others (Mascolo, Fischer, and Neimeyer, 1999; Trevarthen, 1993). Such phenomenal experiences must be carried forward in the development of any reflexive or higher-order representation of self. Thus, one might suggest that selves develop around a phenomenal core that is much like the ubiquitous "center of awareness" that Geertz (1979) rejects.

However, although selves may develop around a phenomenal core, selves cannot be reduced to such cores. As has been suggested here, the self develops with the capacity to direct consciousness upon itself using social symbols that have their origins in culturally framed joint action. As individuals appropriate social meanings to represent the self, selves undergo transformation in the direction of culturally valued endpoints. Further, such reflexive and higher-order representations of self exert downward control over experience and action (Carver and Scheier, 1998; Mascolo and Fischer, 1998). In this way, culture completes the development of self. Although all selves are built upon a phenomenal core of action and experience, they nonetheless undergo dramatic transformation as they develop toward different cultural ideals.

Thinking of the development of self as a process may provide a framework for resolving tensions among different views on the relation between self and culture. The central point is that individuals and cultures are inseparable as causal processes in development. Individuals bring primary experiences to a given social encounter; however, culture is necessary to complete the development of the self, even as it develops around a phenomenal core. In this way, individuality and communality are necessarily represented in the experience and representation of self in all cultures in one form or another. The question is not how culture affects individual development, but how individual and culture necessarily coact in forming the sense of self.

References

Abu-Lughod, L. "Writing Against Culture." In R. D. Fox (ed.), *Recapturing Anthropology: Working in the Present.* Santa Fe, N.M.: School of American Research Press, 1991.

Bond, M. H., and Smith, P. B. "Cross-Cultural Social and Organizational Psychology." *Annual Review of Psychology,* 1996, *47,* 205–235.

Bruner, J., and Kalmar, J. "Narrative and Metanarrative in the Construction of Self." In M. Ferrari and R. Sternberg (eds.), *Self-Awareness.* New York: Guilford Press, 1998.

Carver, C. S., and Scheier, M. F. *On the Self-Regulation of Behavior.* Cambridge: Cambridge University Press, 1998.

Cole, M. *Cultural Psychology: A Once and Future Discipline.* Cambridge, Mass.: Belknap Press, 1996.

Cooley, C. H. *Human Nature and the Social Order* (rev. ed.). New York: Scribner, 1902.

Corsaro, W. *Friendship and Peer Culture in the Early Years.* Norwood, N.J.: Ablex, 1985.

Damon, W., and Hart, D. *Self-Understanding in Childhood and Adolescence.* Cambridge: Cambridge University Press, 1988.

D'Angrade, R. G. *The Development of Cognitive Anthropology.* Cambridge: Cambridge University Press, 1995.

de Munck, V. C. *Culture, Self and Meaning.* Prospect Heights, Ill.: Waveland Press, 2000.

de Rivera, J., and Sarbin, T. R. (eds.). *Believed-in Imaginings: The Narrative Construction of Reality.* Washington, D.C.: American Psychological Association, 1998.

Emde, R. N. "The Prerepresentational Self and Its Affective Core." *Psychoanalytic Study of the Child,* 1983, *38,* 165–192.

Fischer, K. W., and Hogan, A. "The Big Picture for Infant Development: Levels and Variations." In J. Lockman and N. Hazen (eds.), *Action in Social Context: Perspectives on Early Development.* New York: Plenum, 1989.

Fogel, A. *Developing Through Relationships.* Chicago: University of Chicago Press, 1993.

Geertz, C. *The Interpretation of Culture.* New York: Basic Books, 1973.

Gergen, K. J. *The Saturated Self.* New York: Basic Books, 1992.

Gottlieb, G. *Synthesizing Nature-Nurture: Prenatal Roots of Instinctive Behavior.* Mahwah, N.J.: Erlbaum, 1997.

Harre, R. *Personal Being: A Theory for Individual Psychology.* Oxford: Blackwell, 1983.

Harre, R., and Gillett, G. *The Discursive Mind.* Thousand Oaks, Calif.: Sage, 1994.

Harter, S. *The Construction of the Self: A Developmental Perspective.* New York: Guilford Press, 1999.

Hermans, H.J.M., and Kempen, H.J.G. *The Dialogical Self: Meaning as Movement.* Orlando, Fla.: Academic Press, 1993.

James, W. *Principles of Psychology.* New York: Dover, 1890.

Kihlstrom, J. F., Beer, J. S., and Klein, S. B. "Self and Identity as Memory." In M. R. Leary and J. Tangney (eds.), *Handbook of Self and Identity.* New York: Guilford Press, 2002.

Legerstee, M. "Mental and Bodily Awareness in Infancy: Consciousness of Self-Existence." In S. Gallagher and J. Shear (eds.), *Models of the Self.* Thorverton, UK: Imprint Academic, 1999.

Lewis, M. "The Development of Intentionality and the Role of Consciousness." *Psychological Inquiry,* 1990, *1,* 231–248.

Lewis, M., Alessandri, S., and Sullivan, M. W. "Violation of Expectancy, Loss of Control, and Anger in Young Infants." *Developmental Psychology,* 1990, *26,* 745–751.

Lewis, M., and Brooks-Gunn, J. "Self Knowledge and Emotional Development." In M. Lewis and L. Rosenblum (eds.), *The Development of Affect: The Genesis of Behavior.* New York: Plenum, 1978.

Mascolo, M. F., and Fischer, K. W. "The Development of Self Through the Coordination of Component Systems." In M. Ferrari and R. Sternberg (eds.), *Self-Awareness: Its Nature and Development.* New York: Guilford Press, 1998.

Mascolo, M. F., Fischer, K. W., and Li, J. "Dynamic Development of Component Systems of Emotions: Pride, Shame and Guilt in China and the United States." In R. J. Davidson, K. Scherer, and H. H. Goldsmith (eds.), *Handbook of Affective Science.* New York: Oxford University Press, 2003.

Mascolo, M. F., Fischer, K. W., and Neimeyer, R. "The Dynamic Co-Development of Intentionality, Self and Social Relations." In J. Brandstadter and R. M. Lerner (eds.), *Action and Development: Origins and Functions of Intentional Self-Development.* Thousand Oaks, Calif.: Sage, 1999.

Mascolo, M. F., and Harkins, D. "Toward a Component Systems Approach to Emotional Development." In M. F. Mascolo and S. Griffin (eds.), *What Develops in Emotional Development?* New York: Plenum, 1998.

McAdams, D. P. *Narratives We Live by.* New York: Guilford Press, 1993.

Mead, G. H. *Mind, Self and Society from the Standpoint of a Social Behaviorist.* Chicago: University of Chicago, 1932.

Meltzoff, A. N. "The Centrality of Motor Coordination and Proprioception in Social and Cognitive Development: From Shared Actions to Shared Minds." In G.J.P. Savelsbergh (ed.), *The Development of Coordination in Infancy.* New York: Elsevier, 1993.

Merleau-Ponty, M. *Phenomenology of Perception.* London: Routledge and Kegan Paul, 1962. (Originally published 1945)

Moshman, D. *Adolescent Psychological Development: Rationality, Morality, and Identity.* Mahwah, N.J.: Erlbaum, 1999.

Searle, J. *Intentionality.* Cambridge: Cambridge University Press, 1983.

Shotter, J. "The Social Construction of Our 'Inner' Lives." *Journal of Constructivist Psychology,* 1997, *10,* 7–24.

Shweder, R. *Thinking Through Culture: Expeditions in Cultural Psychology.* Cambridge, Mass.: Harvard University Press, 1991.

Shweder, R., and Sullivan, M. "Cultural Psychology: Who Needs It?" *Annual Review of Psychology,* 1993, *44,* 497–523.

Spiro, M. E. "Collective Representations and Mental Representations in Religious Symbol Systems." In B. Kilborne and L. Langness (eds.), *Culture and Human Nature: Theoretical Papers of Melford E. Spiro.* Chicago: University of Chicago Press, 1987.

Stern, D. *The Interpersonal World of the Infant.* New York: Basic Books, 1985.

Strauss, C., and Quinn, N. *A Cognitive Theory of Cultural Meanings.* Cambridge: Cambridge University Press, 1997.
Trevarthen, C. "The Functions of Emotions in Early Infant Communication and Development." In J. Nadel and L. Camaioni (eds.), *New Perspectives in Early Communication Development.* London: Routledge, 1993.
Triandis, H. C. *Culture and Social Behavior.* New York: McGraw-Hill, 1994.

MICHAEL F. MASCOLO is professor of psychology at Merrimack College in North Andover, Massachusetts.

6

Although the constructs of individualism and collectivism appear to bring explanatory power to analyses of culture and psychology, they fail to adequately account for the complexities of social interactions and the multiplicity of people's social judgments. The research considered in the chapters in this volume offers evidence for the need to go beyond the stereotyping of cultures as individualistic or collectivistic.

Commentary: Beyond Individualism and Collectivism—A Problem, or Progress?

Elliot Turiel

For a number of years during the latter part of the twentieth century a movement has emerged, termed "cultural psychology," that takes different forms. For some (Markus and Kitayama, 1991; Triandis, 1989), a focus on culture is closely linked to the proposition that cultures can be divided into those that are predominantly "individualistic" (usually in the Western side of the world) and those that are predominantly "collectivistic" (usually in the East). One of the tenets of some proponents of cultural psychology is that culture, with its traditions and practices, regulates and constitutes the human psyche and constitutes psychological make-up itself (for an alternative view, see Cole, 1997). Another central tenet is that cultures have their own "logic," so to speak, and therefore can and often do differ from each other. It is the quest for a system of logic or organization within cultures that is linked to the purported discoveries that in the social and personality realms two distinguishable types can be identified and neatly labeled: individualism and collectivism. They encompass differences in personal identity, conceptions of self and persons, the nature of social relationships, and moral values and judgments.

There are several distinct advantages to these propositions—as perceived by their proponents. For one, they provide an attractive alternative to those approaches, especially sociobiology and evolutionary psychology, that look to explain behavior, thought, personality, and morality through genetic and evolutionary processes. The fixed and universal characteristics presumed in biologically based explanations are replaced by variable,

NEW DIRECTIONS FOR CHILD AND ADOLESCENT DEVELOPMENT, no. 104, Summer 2004 © Wiley Periodicals, Inc.

contextualized, and culturally based ones. Second, the propositions of cultural psychology support ways of describing differences between nations, religions, ethnic groups, and socioeconomic groups. We can call it culture. Third, they lend coherence to apparent variations in people's thought and action by giving an explanation of how some people come to function in certain systematic ways that differ from the systematic ways some other people function (that is, by living in a particular locale). The main advantage here is that explanatory order is established. Fourth, the propositions of individualism and collectivism yield the substance of those modes of functioning through descriptions of how people in different places with different histories seem to think so differently about themselves and moral matters. An orientation to the person as a free being with entitlements, autonomy, and independence, which we see in the Western world, makes for a morality that differs from the morality we see in non-Western settings where the orientation is to people as part of a social network (the group) with interpersonal obligations, duties, and interdependence. The key here is that non-Westerners think very differently from Westerners about the person; the person is not a bounded entity in the non-Western conception, which diverges from the Western view of the person as bounded and separate from other people. Divergent conceptions of the person, social interactions, and morality involve uniformities; within cultures beliefs are shared and agreements exist.

There is at least one distinct disadvantage, however, to the characterization of cultures as individualistic or collectivist: it is likely to be false, and it serves thereby to stereotype people and groups. A number of years ago, some of my own research on moral and social development was influenced by the apparent falseness of central propositions regarding individualism and collectivism. It seemed to me that the idea was patently false for one simple reason: most groups (societies, cultures, or whatever we choose to call groups) are structured hierarchically (especially in accordance with distributions of power by socioeconomic class and gender) and people in positions of power in those hierarchies are often highly "individualistic." By this I mean that, for example, men in patriarchal cultures have a strong sense of autonomy, independence, personal entitlement, and freedom of choice. Men especially assert their autonomy in relationships with women. Such hierarchical structures are enmeshed in those cultures labeled collectivistic (or nonindividualistic). As one adolescent female living in a patriarchal society (a relatively isolated Druze community in Israel) put it in responding to questions used in some of our research on these matters (Turiel and Wainryb, 2000, p. 252): "in our culture a man is given complete freedom. . . . No one would oppose a man being free." An adolescent male in the same community also espoused these sentiments: "A man needs to be free, he's supposed to be free." He went on to say that a woman "is under his [that is, her husband's] control. Either her parents dominate her or her husband does" (pp. 252–253).

COMMENTARY: BEYOND INDIVIDUALISM AND COLLECTIVISM   93

The research that yielded responses of this type is part of a broader program of research (Mensing, 2002; Neff, 2001; Turiel, 2002; Turiel and Wainryb, 1998; Wainryb, 1995; Wainryb and Turiel, 1994) that has pursued the idea that individualism is alive and kicking in cultures in which one group (for instance, males) holds greater power and status than another (females). Consistent with the research presented in the chapters in this volume, our research demonstrated that in non-Western and Western cultures there are complex mixtures of the features supposedly falling within collectivism and individualism. Indeed, it is necessary to go beyond individualism and collectivism to analyses of the multiplicity of selves within and between cultures.

In reflecting upon the informative and well-reasoned set of chapters in this volume, I was reminded of a comment made to me a few years ago when I presented some of these ideas and research findings to a group of psychologists. A very well-informed and experienced researcher said that he was sorry to say that he agreed with me. I must confess that his comment initially took me aback since I did not grasp his intent and worried that it was directed at me personally. I asked him to explain. He said he agreed with my analyses and found the evidence compelling but was sorry to "admit" it because it eliminated what he had thought was one of the few descriptions of social behaviors that brought coherence and explanatory power to psychology. He added that the field had little in the way of explanatory power and that undermining the characterizations of cultures and the social lives of people as individualistic and collectivistic removed one of the few available possibilities. In other words, he recognized that one of the advantages I noted of these characterizations would be taken away.

I believe two ideas were behind the general reaction. One is that culture is key to explaining social behaviors and social interactions. It follows that if cultures were coherent and could be characterized by a global organization, we would be able to explain people's social behaviors. I also believe that these two presumptions are incorrect and that social interactions and behaviors can be understood without resorting to global characterizations (stereotypes) of cultures and their members. Alternative propositions about individuals, development, and their intersections are in order. Development entails a process of the individual's interactions with a multifaceted social world that includes a variety of social interactions. In turn, individuals form a variety of perspectives and judgments and can be at odds with, or critical of, their cultural practices. The chapters in this volume are consistent with these propositions, and the research findings presented show that we can examine variations in the context of coherence in thoughts, feelings, and social relationships. The research demonstrates, as I would put it (see Turiel, 2003, and Turiel and Perkins, forthcoming), that we need to attend to flexibilities of mind and not lock people into boxes supposedly framed by cultural orientations. With flexibility of mind, people in all cultures typically apply, in purposeful ways, their evaluations and judgments to the particularities of social contexts. Social contexts need to be specified at levels narrower than the broad cultural context.

As I interpret it, the work presented in this volume was conducted by each of the researchers with deliberate efforts to avoid imposing the templates or stereotypes that can come from preordained categories. Each researcher employed the strategy of being open to viewing the data in ways other than through the lens of features attributed to individualism and collectivism. The chapters have important common themes about people's thinking and what occurs within cultures. These themes are captured by the common use of terms such as *coexistence, multifaceted, domain differences,* and *context.* There are a coexistence of autonomy and connectedness, multifaceted views of self and social relationships, and differences in judgments by the domain of endeavor; the coexisting, multifaceted views are applied in different ways in different contexts.

I believe that these propositions are strongly supported by the evidence presented in all the chapters. Akiba, Szalacha, and García Coll, the only ones who do not directly address individualism and collectivism, nevertheless make the same general point by demonstrating that even ethnic identity is a multidimensional concept. They argue that singular concepts of identity (which would also apply to cultural identity) are inadequate in capturing the connections of identities to other dimensions, such as gender and role. Mascolo, Misra, and Rapisardi report a comparative study conducted in urban areas in India and the United States. Their examination of representations of self on the part of people in those two settings revealed that both groups are concerned with social relationships and interdependence, as well as the self and freedom. One of their striking findings is that Americans spoke more in terms of mutuality than Indians did. At the surface, this may seem paradoxical since Americans are supposed to be individualistic, whereas Indians are supposed to be collectivistic. These findings illustrate that additional social factors need to be taken into account to understand how people think about social relationships. The relevant feature here is that Indian society is structured hierarchically to a greater extent than American society. The equality in American society produces lesser constraints on mutuality than the social hierarchy of Indian society. This does not mean, however, that a hierarchical structure prevents Indians from being concerned with relationships. As Mascolo, Misra, and Rapisardi stress, concerns with relationships take different forms. A question that arises from the findings of relatively little expression of mutuality in a hierarchical setting is whether people—especially those in lesser positions of power—nevertheless strive for greater mutuality. I return to this question later. However, the findings by Mascolo and colleagues that Indians expressed feelings of freedom suggest that autonomy, and by extension mutuality, is part of Indians' conceptualizations of self and social relationships.

It is also striking that the findings contrast with elements of traditional Indian philosophy that Mascolo and coauthors discuss. The findings indicate, first, that there may be discrepancies between public ideologies and what people believe or how they think. In turn, this would suggest that people's thinking is based as much on their direct experiences (if not more so) as on their exposure to public ideologies. People do not simply incorporate the tenets of public pronouncements but interpret them. These propositions are also supported by research by Spiro (1993) in Burma. He was able to determine that the Burmese maintain conceptions of self that include a subjective sense of ego, which is denied in a central doctrine of Theravada Buddhism. As Spiro interprets it, the doctrine is not entirely incorporated by the Burmese villagers because it is discrepant with their direct experiences of a subjective sense of self.

Moreover, it is likely that in the original, as well as in their transformations over time, public ideologies or traditional philosophies are multifaceted. This is clearly brought out by Li and Yue in their discussion of Confucianism. As they put it, scholars find space for the individual and autonomy in Confucianism, and the view of Confucianism as mainly deemphasizing the individual is one-sided (see Nussbaum, 2000, and Sen, 1997, for similar accounts about Indian philosophies). Not only are public doctrines multifaceted, but also different people (scholars included) make various interpretations of the same documents.

In any event, Li and Yue show that conceptions of self and autonomy are strong in the orientations of Chinese adolescents. By focusing on the domain of learning, they tapped into a type of activity that is inherently connected to self-enhancement and agency. Indeed, they point out that personal goals and agency are consistent with Confucian teachings about learning. At least two important lessons can be derived from the approach taken by Li and Yue. One is that Chinese adolescents cannot be seen as adhering to any type of general social orientation. The second pertains to something of a sampling issue—sampling of realms of activity. Li and Yue purposefully chose to study the domain of learning, correctly presuming that it would be likely to pull for concepts of autonomy and agency. They showed that such concepts stand alongside the previously documented concepts of connectedness among Indians. Their research shows that unless a variety of domains or realms of activity are included in research, the findings will be misleading.

Indeed, there is a sense in which Indians appear more individualistic than Americans if we compare the findings obtained by Li and Yue with those obtained by Raeff. Whereas Li and Yue found more of an individual orientation than a social orientation among Indians, Raeff found an interweaving of the two in Americans. I do not mean to imply that Indians are more individualistic than Americans. Rather, I want to stress that there is an intersection between people's thinking and domains. Such an intersection shows that the application of concepts of autonomy or relatedness is not solely due to culturally based categories; it reflects the active interpretations people make about events they experience.

It is interesting that Raeff found a combination of autonomy and connectedness among those who are often seen as some of the most independent, contrary, and individualistic in the world: American adolescents. She also found the interweaving of the orientations even though the adolescents in her study were asked general questions (such as, "Tell me about yourself" and "How would you describe yourself?"). It is likely that further complexity and heterogeneity on the individualism-collectivism dimension would be evident if questions were posed about different realms of activity and within specified contexts of relationships. Consider these examples. The types of questions posed by Raeff can be extended by saying, "Tell me about yourself when you do such and such [insert a learning context, a work context, a family context, a game context, and so on]." The same can be done for the question, "How would you describe yourself?"

Another way of contextualizing the questions would be to place them in particular relationships: "Tell me about yourself when you are with X [insert a parent, a sibling, a friend, a teacher, an employer, an employee, and so forth]." With any of these targeted individuals, the context can be considered in terms of the equality or inequality of the relationship. For instance, would it matter if the other person were in a dominant or subordinate position in the social hierarchy relative to the respondent (on the basis of social class, gender, or the characteristics of the individuals)? As suggested by both theoretical considerations (Nussbaum, 1999, 2000; Okin, 1989; Turiel, 2002; Wikan, 1991) and research findings (Abu-Lughod, 1993; Wainryb and Turiel, 1994; Wikan, 1996), examining judgments about contexts shows that people experience ambivalence, contradiction, conflict, opposition, and subversion.

The existence of conflict and opposition to cultural practices suggests that some of the bedrocks of cultural analyses require modification. I am referring particularly to the ideas that cultures are defined by shared beliefs and social harmony (Triandis, 1989). On that basis, philosophers, anthropologists, and psychologists recently have criticized the types of portrayal of culture as homogeneous that leads to conceptions such as individualism and collectivism. For instance, Martha Nussbaum, a philosopher who has written about the perspectives of women in developing countries, put it this way: "Cultures are not monoliths; people are not stamped out like coins by the power machine of social convention. They are constrained by social norms, but norms are plural and people are devious. Even in societies that nourish problematic roles for men and women, real men and women can find spaces in which to subvert those conventions. Customs and political arrangements are important pauses of women's misery and death" (1999, p. 32).

Insofar as customs, social arrangements, and cultural practices are causes of women's misery or suffering, it is not to be expected that women will simply accept those ways. As articulated by Susan Okin, disagreements are the rule in such situations: "Oppressors and oppressed—when the voice of the latter can be heard at all—often disagree fundamentally. . . . Contemporary views about gender are a clear example of such disagreements; it is clear that there are no shared understandings on this subject, even among women" (1989, p. 67).

When Okin stated that the voices of the oppressed are not heard often, she was referring to their voices within societies. She could just as well have noted that the voices of the oppressed, the poor, and more generally those in nondominant positions in the social hierarchy are not heard by researchers. Researchers, including psychologists and anthropologists, usually portray cultural orientations from the perspective of those in positions of power. According to Wikan (1991), the nearly exclusive study of such groups renders it easier to characterize cultures as entailing shared beliefs and social harmony at the expense of the conflicts, opposition, and struggles that commonly occur: "They were the vocal ones, the eloquent, the experts we sought out while the poor, the infirm, women and youth were disregarded as uninformed about "truth". . . . And so it is [that] the concept of culture as a seamless whole and of society as a bounded group manifesting inherently valued order and normatively regulated response, effectively masked human misery and quenched dissenting voices" (p. 290).

Let me give one example to illustrate Wikan's point. It comes from research Cecilia Wainryb and I (Wainryb and Turiel, 1994) conducted with males and females in a patriarchal culture (a Druze Arab community). This is one of the studies I mentioned earlier that were designed to ascertain if people in positions of power have a sense of autonomy. We did find that males maintain they should have freedoms, which are not granted to females. Both males and females tended to portray females as required to fulfill their role obligations and be oriented to social relationships. In an effort to tap into the perspectives of females on cultural practices that grant power and control to males, we asked them to morally evaluate those practices. It turned out that the large majority of females (adolescents and adults) judged the practices and social arrangements to be unfair.

That females judged practices central to a patriarchal system unfair is contrary to the idea that people's morality is governed by cultural norms or traditional philosophies; most important for the present purposes, it indicates that there is an undercurrent of discontent with the roles that women have in a system of interdependence—as far as females are concerned. The findings of that study actually undermine two facets of collectivism as an overarching orientation of the culture: autonomy and independence are part of their thinking and people are critical of the inequalities imposed on them. The findings also demonstrated the importance of examining the perspectives of those in nondominant positions, as stressed by Nussbaum, Okin, and Wikan. Some anthropologists, such as Wikan (1996) and Abu-Lughod (1993), have studied the activities of women and the poor when faced with restrictions they consider unfair. Both observed a good deal of opposition to, and subversion of, cultural practices in people's daily lives. Abu-Lughod, for instance, found that Bedouin women in Egypt regularly engage in actions to avoid and transform unequal restrictions imposed upon them with regard to education, work, and marriage.

There are suggestions in this volume, as well, that differences exist between groups within cultures. Li and Yue report gender differences in the goals expressed in the realm of learning. Li (2001) has previously reported findings of social class differences in learning goals and personal agency. Chinese children and adolescents from lower socioeconomic groups were more likely than those from higher socioeconomic groups to express individual goals and concerns with autonomy. The findings may be surprising to those who expect that people of higher social classes are more "individualistic" (see Li, 2001). The findings are not surprising, however, from the viewpoint that people strive to change their lot in life. By that interpretation, the Chinese from lower socioeconomic groups set goals of learning for themselves as a means of improving their condition, overcoming adversity, and gaining greater control over their lives.

Ultimately, all these considerations—and this volume as a whole—raise issues about the very concept of culture. Going beyond individualism and collectivism raises difficult issues since we are left with multiplicity in conceptions of selves within and between cultures, variations among contexts within cultures, and even opposition to culture, with attempts to transform it, on the part of those who at the same time identify with their culture. As all the authors in this volume make abundantly clear, these complexities render the constructs of individualism and collectivism problematic. The multiplicity of perspectives within cultures has led to serious consideration, especially among anthropologists, of the concept of culture and whether it should be retained in the discipline (see Wikan, 2002, for a discussion of these matters). Abu-Lughod (1991) provocatively titled one of her essays "Writing Against Culture," proclaiming that the "notion of culture (especially as it functions to distinguish 'cultures'), despite a long usefulness, may now have become something that anthropologists would want to work against in their theories, their ethnographic practices, and their ethnographic writing" (p. 138). Abu-Lughod was vague (perhaps purposefully) as to whether we should do away with the term. However, she was not at all vague about the problems in how the term has been used: "By focusing closely on particular individuals and their changing relationships, one would necessarily subvert the most problematic connotations of culture: homogeneity, coherence, and timelessness. Individuals are confronted with choices, struggle with others, make conflicting statements, argue about points of view on the same events, undergo ups and downs in various relationships and changes in their circumstances, and fail to predict what will happen to them or those around them" (1991, p, 154).

It seems to me that the authors of the chapters in this volume are largely in agreement with Abu-Lughod's contentions about the problematic connotations of culture, even if they might disagree with her views about working against culture in their theories. They would probably agree with Wikan (2002, p. 88), who stated that the use of the term *culture,* in some instances at least, "covers up the complexity of human existence, the fact that we are both children of 'our culture' and unique individuals." If we agree with Abu-Lughod when she states that individuals struggle with others, are involved in conflicts, and argue with each other, then descriptions of orientations such as individualism and collectivism give us a coherence that is discrepant with reality.

Those descriptions also give us a coherence that only appears less fixed than those provided by the biologically based explanations. Whereas descriptions of individualism and collectivism do attempt to account for variations between cultures, they imply that people follow a template that is consistent with what is given culturally. Rather than recognizing the flexibility of mind people bring to a social world that includes a variety of perspectives and problems, people are seen as locked into a cultural script. Children's development, as Piaget ([1951] 1995) clearly articulated, entails the construction of flexible thought through interactions with multiple types of social experiences.

References

Abu-Lughod, L. "Writing Against Culture." In R. E. Fox (ed.), *Recapturing Anthropology: Working in the Present.* Santa Fe, N.M.: School of American Research Press, 1991.

Abu-Lughod, L. *Writing Women's Worlds: Bedouin Stories.* Berkeley: University of California Press, 1993.

Cole, M. *Cultural Psychology: A Once and Future Discipline.* Cambridge, Mass.: Harvard University Press, 1997.

Li, J. "Individual Self and Social Self in Learning Among Chinese Adolescents." Paper presented at the Biennial Meeting of the Society for Research in Child Development, Minneapolis, Apr. 2001.

Markus, H. R., and Kitayama, S. "Culture and Self: Implications for Cognition, Emotion, and Motivation." *Psychological Review,* 1991, *98,* 224–253.

Mensing, J. F. "Collectivism, Individualism, and Interpersonal Responsibilities in Families: Differences and Similarities in Social Reasoning Between Individuals in Poor, Urban Families in Colombia and the United States." Unpublished doctoral dissertation, University of California, Berkeley, 2002.

Neff, K. D. "Judgments of Personal Autonomy and Interpersonal Responsibility in the Context of Indian Spousal Relationships: An Examination of Young People's Reasoning in Mysore, India." *British Journal of Developmental Psychology,* 2001, *19,* 233–257.

Nussbaum, M. C. *Sex and Social Justice.* New York: Oxford University Press, 1999.

Nussbaum, M. C. *Women and Human Development: The Capabilities Approach.* Cambridge: Cambridge University Press, 2000.

Okin, S. M. *Justice, Gender, and the Family.* New York: Basic Books, 1989.

Piaget, J. "Egocentric Thought and Sociocentric Thought." In J. Piaget, *Sociological Studies.* London: Routledge, 1995. (Originally published 1951)

Sen, A. "Human Rights and Asian Values." *New Republic,* July 14 and 21, 1997, pp. 33–39.

Spiro, M. "Is the Western Conception of the Self 'Peculiar' Within the Context of the World Cultures?" *Ethos,* 1993, *21,* 107–153.

Triandis, H. C. "The Self and Social Behavior in Differing Cultural Contexts." *Psychological Review*, 1989, *96*, 506–520.

Turiel, E. *The Culture of Morality: Social Development, Context, and Conflict.* Cambridge: Cambridge University Press, 2002.

Turiel, E. "Resistance and Subversion in Everyday Life." *Journal of Moral Education*, 2003, *32*, 115–130.

Turiel, E., and Perkins, S. A. "Flexibilities of Mind: Conflict and Culture." *Human Development*, forthcoming.

Turiel, E., and Wainryb, C. "Concepts of Freedoms and Rights in a Traditional Hierarchically Organized Society." *British Journal of Developmental Psychology*, 1998, *16*, 375–395.

Turiel, E., and Wainryb, C. "Social Life in Cultures: Judgments, Conflicts, and Subversion." *Child Development*, 2000, *71*, 250–256.

Wainryb, C. "Reasoning About Social Conflicts in Different Cultures: Druze and Jewish Children in Israel." *Child Development*, 1995, *66*, 390–401.

Wainryb, C., and Turiel, E. "Dominance, Subordination, and Concepts of Personal Entitlements in Cultural Contexts." *Child Development*, 1994, *65*, 1701–1722.

Wikan, U. "Toward an Experience-Near Anthropology." *Cultural Anthropology*, 1991, *6*, 285–305.

Wikan, U. *Tomorrow, God Willing: Self-Made Destinies in Cairo.* Chicago: University of Chicago Press, 1996.

Wikan, U. *Generous Betrayal: Politics of Culture in the New Europe.* Chicago: University of Chicago Press, 2002.

ELLIOT TURIEL *is professor of education at the University of California, Berkeley.*

INDEX

Aboud, F. E., 48, 53, 54
Abu-Lughod, L., 84, 96, 97, 98
Achievement, 29. *See also* Learning
Adolescence, 68
African Americans, 45–46, 47, 48
Agarwal, R., 3
Agency. *See* Personal agency
Akiba, D., 5, 45, 46, 56, 94
Alarcón, O., 50
Alessandri, S., 80, 87
Allocentric selves, 1
American culture. *See* Western culture
Anatta, 12
Anger, 20
Arnold, M. L., 28, 29, 38
Artha, 12
Asian children. *See specific ethnicities*
Atkinson, R., 63
Atman, 10, 11, 12, 22
Authority, 20–22
Autonomy: adhering to preconceived notions of, 72; conflict between connectedness and, 72; definition of, 66, 72; dichotomous conceptualizations of, 61–63; in human development, 63; in patriarchal cultures, 97; reconceptualization of, 64–66; study of, 66–76
Azorean identification, 53

Bankston, C. L., 48
Beer, J. S., 82
Bellah, R. N., 9
Bernal, M. E., 48
von Bertalanffy, L., 76
Bharati, A., 10, 12
Bhatia, S., 13, 24
Biggs, J. B., 29, 30, 37
Blatt, S. J., 63, 65
Bond, M. H., 27, 28, 38, 83
Bourne, E. J., 62–63, 70
Boyd, D., 28, 29, 38
Boys, 39, 68, 71
Bracken, B., 37, 38
Brahmacarya, 10
Brahman, 10, 11, 12, 22
Branch, C., 46, 47
Brooks-Gunn, J., 82
Bruner, J., 82

Buddhist philosophy, 12, 95
Burma, 95

Cambodian children. *See* Children, Cambodian
Carver, C. S., 87
Chand, T., 13
Chang, H. C., 28
Chao, F., 28, 29, 30, 40
Chapman, M., 51
Chavira, V., 48
Cheung, T., 28
Children: and coregulation, 84–86; in Hindu stages of life, 10; in Indian hierarchy, 13, 24
Children, Cambodian, 48–56
Children, Chinese: achievement of, 29; goals of, 31–34; study of, 29–36
Children, Dominican, 48–56
Children, Portuguese, 48–56
Chinese culture: complexity of self in, 37–41; countering views about, 28–29; definition of knowledge in, 30; learning in, 29–41; overview of, 27
Chiu, C.-Y., 28, 29, 30
Civil service, 37
Clark, K. B., 45, 46, 47, 48
Clark, M. P., 45, 46, 47, 48
Cocking, R. R., 1, 4
Cognitive abilities, 74
Cognitive anthropologists, 83
Cole, M., 79, 91
Collectivist cultures: definition of, 1; and patriarchy, 97; self-conceptions in, 23; stereotypes of, 92; view of individual in, 1
Competition, 35, 40
Concentration, 34
Confucianism, 27, 28, 30, 37, 95
Connectedness: adhering to preconceived notions of, 72; conflicts between autonomy and, 72; definition of, 66; dichotomous conceptualizations of, 61–63; in human development, 63; reconceptualization of, 64–66; study of, 66–76
Conscious activity, 80
Content, 37

101

Hernandez Sheets, R., 48
Higher-order representations, 82
Hindu philosophy, 10–13
Ho, D.Y.F., 27, 28, 29, 30
Hofstede, G., 1, 27
Hogan, A., 87
Hong, Y.-Y., 28
hooks, b., 57
Horowitz, R., 45, 46–47
Howard, K. I., 63
Hsu, F.L.K., 27
Huang, L. N., 46
Hui, C., 27, 28, 38
Human development. *See* Development, human
Humility, 34

I self, 65, 82
I-C distinction: definition of, 1; function of, 2; risks in using, 2–3; and study of Chinese children, 38–39
Identity formation, 65
Idiocentric selves, 1
Immigrants, 47, 48–56
Independent variable, culture as, 2
Indian culture: concept of self in, 10–13; duties of family in, 13, 24; multiplicity of selfhood in, 22–25; self-in-relationship study of, 13–22; social values in, 12–13, 24
Indian philosophy, 10–13
Individualist cultures: definition of, 1; self-conceptions in, 23; stereotypes of, 92. *See also* Western culture
Interaction modes, 15, 16, 17. *See also* Social interaction
Interdependence, 23
Intimacy modes, 15, 16, 17
Introverts, 22
Israel, 92

James, W., 64, 82
Johnson, F., 9
Jones, S., 28, 30
Josselson, R., 65

Kagitçibasi, Ç, 2, 29
Kakar, S., 10
Kalmar, J., 82
Kama, 12
Kant, I., 13
Kemmelmeier, M., 1, 63
Kempen, H.J.G., 23, 82
Kihlstrom, J. F., 82

Kim, U., 1, 9
King, A.Y.C., 28
Kirson, D., 31, 32
Kitayama, S., 1, 16, 23, 62, 64, 72, 91
Klein, S. B., 82
Knowledge, definition of, 30
Kohlberg, L., 13

Labels, ethnic, 48–56
Lai, S., 30
Latino people, 46. *See also specific ethnicities*
Lau, S., 28
Learning: in Chinese culture, 29–41; as domain, 38–39; goals of, 32–34; self-concept in, 38. *See also* Achievement
Learning virtues, 30, 39
Leung, K., 28, 38
Lewis, M., 80, 87
Li, J., 4–5, 27, 29, 37, 39, 84, 95, 98
Life stages, 10, 11
Lindenberger, U., 51
Lopez, D., 53

Mahadevan, T.M.P., 10, 12
Marcia, J. E., 47
Marcus, H., 16, 23
Marková, I., 65
Markus, H. J., 1, 30, 62, 64, 72, 91
Marriage, 10
Mascolo, M. F., 4, 6, 9, 13, 24, 79, 80, 82, 84, 85, 87, 94
Material objects, 12
Māyā, 12
McCusker, C., 27, 28, 38
Me self, 64, 82
Mead, G. H., 64–65
Meaning systems, 83–84
Men, 92, 97
Menon, T., 28
Mensing, J. F., 93
Merleau-Ponty, M., 80
Middle childhood: overview of, 45; study of ethnic identity in, 48–56
Miller, J., 12, 13
Mines, M., 63
Misra, G., 2, 3, 4, 9, 94
Mizrahi, K., 49
Moksa, 10, 11, 12
Monsour, A., 14
Morality: in Indian culture, 12–13, 24; in Western culture, 13, 24
Morris, M. W., 28

Back Issue/Subscription Order Form

Copy or detach and send to:

Jossey-Bass, A Wiley Company, 989 Market Street, San Francisco CA 94103-1741

Call or fax toll-free: Phone 888-378-2537 6:30AM – 3PM PST; Fax 888-481-2665

Back Issues: Please send me the following issues at $29 each
(Important: please include series initials and issue number, such as CD99.)

_____

_____

_____

$ _____   Total for single issues

$ _____   SHIPPING CHARGES: SURFACE   Domestic   Canadian

	Domestic	Canadian
First Item	$5.00	$6.00
Each Add'l Item	$3.00	$1.50

For next-day and second-day delivery rates, call the number listed above.

Subscriptions: Please __start __renew my subscription to *New Directions for Child and Adolescent Development* for the year 2____at the following rate:

U.S.	__Individual $90	__Institutional $195
Canada	__Individual $90	__Institutional $235
All Others	__Individual $114	__Institutional $269
Online Subscription		__Institutional $195

**For more information about online subscriptions visit
www.interscience.wiley.com**

$ _____   Total single issues and subscriptions (Add appropriate sales tax for your state for single issue orders. No sales tax for U.S. subscriptions. Canadian residents, add GST for subscriptions and single issues.)

__Payment enclosed (U.S. check or money order only)

__VISA __MC __AmEx # _____   Exp. Date _____

Signature _____ Day Phone _____

__ Bill Me (U.S. institutional orders only. Purchase order required.)

Purchase order # _____
        Federal Tax ID13559302   GST 89102 8052

Name _____

Address _____

_____

Phone _____ E-mail _____

For more information about Jossey-Bass, visit our Web site at **www.josseybass.com**

OTHER TITLES AVAILABLE IN THE
NEW DIRECTIONS FOR CHILD AND ADOLESCENT DEVELOPMENT SERIES
William Damon, Editor-in-Chief

**NEW DIRECTIONS FOR
CHILD AND ADOLESCENT DEVELOPMENT
IS NOW AVAILABLE ONLINE AT WILEY INTERSCIENCE**

What is Wiley InterScience?

Wiley InterScience is the dynamic online content service from John Wiley & Sons delivering the full text of over 300 leading scientific, technical, medical, and professional journals, plus major reference works, the acclaimed Current Protocols laboratory manuals, and even the full text of select Wiley print books online.

What are some special features of Wiley InterScience?

Wiley Interscience Alerts is a service that delivers table of contents via e-mail for any journal available on Wiley InterScience as soon as a new issue is published online.
EarlyView is Wiley's exclusive service presenting individual articles online as soon as they are ready, even before the release of the compiled print issue. These articles are complete, peer-reviewed, and citable.
CrossRef is the innovative multi-publisher reference linking system enabling readers to move seamlessly from a reference in a journal article to the cited publication, typically located on a different server and published by a different publisher.

How can I access Wiley InterScience?

Visit http://www.interscience.wiley.com.

Guest Users can browse Wiley InterScience for unrestricted access to journal tables of contents and article abstracts, or use the powerful search engine.
Registered Users are provided with a *Personal Home Page* to store and manage customized alerts, searches, and links to favorite journals and articles. Additionally, Registered Users can view free online sample issues and preview selected material from major reference works.
Licensed Customers are entitled to access full-text journal articles in PDF, with select journals also offering full-text HTML.

How do I become an Authorized User?

Authorized Users are individuals authorized by a paying Customer to have access to the journals in Wiley InterScience. For example, a university that subscribes to Wiley journals is considered to be the Customer. Faculty, staff and students authorized by the university to have access to those journals in Wiley InterScience are Authorized Users. Users should contact their library for information on which Wiley journals they have access to in Wiley InterScience.

ASK YOUR INSTITUTION ABOUT WILEY INTERSCIENCE TODAY!